SINCE
YOU
ASKED

SINCE YOU ASKED

Answers to Questions Asked by Readers of The Lutheran

Norma Cook Everist and Burton L. Everist

Augsburg ∎ Minneapolis

SINCE YOU ASKED
Answers to Questions Asked by Readers of *The Lutheran*

Scripture quotations unless otherwise noted are the authors' translations.

Scripture quotations marked RSV are from the Revised Standard Version of the Bible, copyright © 1946, 1952, and 1971 by the Division of Christian Education of the National Council of Churches.

Cover design: Lecy Design

Library of Congress Cataloging-in-Publication Data

Everist, Norma J.
    Since you asked : answers to questions asked by readers of the
Lutheran / Norma and Burton Everist.
        p.   cm.
    ISBN 0-8066-2439-6.
    1. Evangelical Lutheran Church in America—Doctrines—Miscellanea.
2. Lutheran Church—Doctrines—Miscellanea.   3. Lutheran (Chicago,
Ill. : 1988)   I. Everist, Burton, 1937–   II. Title.
BX8065.2.E94   1989
284.1'35—dc20   89-36049
                                                                    CIP

The paper used in this publication meets the minimum requirements of American National Standard for Information Sciences—Permanence of Paper for Printed Library Materials, ANSI Z329.48-1984. ∞™

Manufactured in the U.S.A.   AF 9-2439

93   92   91   90   89   1   2   3   4   5   6   7   8   9   10

Contents

job and since clergy don't pay taxes?—39 ▪ Should a congregation pay for their pastor's doctorate?—41 ▪ What has become of deaconesses?—41 ▪ Who are Associates in Ministry?—44

3 Life Together in the Congregation   46

What can we do about the noise in the narthex?—46 ▪ Should people simply drop children off at the church door for Sunday school?—47 ▪ Are there any youth programs beyond bake sales and car washes?—48 ▪ Is a large church wedding proper for a couple who each have been married and divorced?—49 ▪ Does our church have guidelines concerning the makeup of church councils, specifically the male-female balance?—51 ▪ Should members of our congregation who spend the winter in a warmer climate be active in the decision-making process when away?—52 ▪ I visited a nearby church, and the pastor came to call. Was he recruiting?—54 ▪ Does a sign that simply shows a saint's name and the words, "A Lutheran Parish Community," really say who we are?—55 ▪ Are craft fairs in the church appropriate?—56 ▪ Should our congregation hold a raffle?—57 ▪ Should we contribute to endowment funds to safeguard our congregation's future?—58

4 Interpretations of the Scriptures   60

How can the Evangelical Lutheran Church in America ordain women in the light of 1 Timothy 2:11-15?—60 ▪ Is it now considered naive or even heresy to believe that Adam and Eve were real people?—64 ▪ Has the Lutheran church examined the books of the Apocrypha?—66 ▪ Why do the Psalms differ in the hymnals of the Evangelical Lutheran Church in America and the Lutheran Church–Missouri Synod?—68 ▪ What is the "unforgiveable sin"?—68 ▪ How can we overcome Bible study boredom?—70 ▪ How do we help people see Bible stories as more than morality tales?—71

5 Issues concerning Theological Beliefs   73

Whatever happened to the definition of God from Luther's *Small Catechism*?—74 ▪ Was Jesus born to die?—75 ▪ What does "being saved" mean for Lutherans?—77 ▪ Why has *Christian* been changed to *catholic* in the creed?—79 ■ We know *catholic* means "universal," but how does that guarantee everything is Christian?—80 ■ Is the priesthood of all believers or universalism the basis of an inclusive church?—81 ■ Are private Baptisms a good idea?—82 ■ Why doesn't the Lutheran church talk or say more about the second coming of Jesus Christ?—83 ■ Why is the Athanasian Creed in the *Lutheran Book of Worship?*—85 ■ There are rumors in my congregation that the Evangelical Lutheran Church in America believes in universalism, does not believe in the virgin birth, the resurrection, or in the inerrancy of the Bible. Is this true?—86

Introduction

People learn best when they receive responses to their own questions. The questions in this book come from church members who submitted them to our column, "Since You Asked," in *The Lutheran*. These questions, which are arranged by topic, can stimulate discussion in homes, Bible classes, or open forums. The question and response format has evoked lively discussions among readers. Some of those responses are included in this book to further the dialog—something space does not allow in the magazine. The question format and the topical arrangement will help promote healthy discussion and helpful learning in your community of faith.

Chapter Contents

Chapter 1 centers on worship, an area in which we continuously receive much mail. The questions concern not only liturgical practice, but also the ways a Christian community goes about making changes. Because worship is the single place where members of congregations are together regularly, it is not surprising that questions of what it means to be the people of God together would focus on worship form and content. Other dimensions of "being the church" are more abstract and diverse, although equally important.

One such dimension is the relationship between congregation members and their pastors and Associates in Ministry. Chapter 2 deals with church leadership. The shifting of pastoral roles is repeatedly addressed in questions that demonstrate highly differing expectations in leadership and decision making. Members are ambivalent, wishing to claim their authority and yet

expecting their pastor to be a strong leader. Although these relationship issues are abstract, they are played out in concrete,
everyday experience.

Members in a congregation hold a whole range of opinions:
One says children need to be closely supervised, another says
they should be allowed their freedom. One says couples should
save money for retirement, another says that money could be
given for hunger relief. A healthy congregation welcomes such
diversity and tries to discern what it means to be the body of
Christ. Therefore, chapter 3 addresses life together in the congregation. Its content is arranged to show how we change and
yet how we need each other at various stages of the life cycle.

Chapter 4 responds to the many questions referring to
biblical authority and interpretation. There is, quite obviously, a
range of biblical perspectives in the Lutheran church. The chapter's goal is not to narrow the scope, but to deepen the discussion
and to encourage continued communal use of the Bible in the
congregation as well as in private, devotional reading.

Then we move from biblical bases to theological foundations. In chapter 5, the questions are arranged according to
articles in the Augsburg Confession, a document Lutherans affirm
but rarely read for themselves. The excerpts may stimulate people
to read further in *The Book of Concord*. The everyday actions of
people are "theological" in that they deal with brokenness and
new life, our relationship to God and to each other. We do well
to engage regularly in such theological reflection. The questions
in this chapter help people do that.

Chapter 6 includes letters about relationships with other
faith bodies. Relationships with the Roman Catholic Church and
also with the Lutheran Church–Missouri Synod concerned many
readers. A few questions address world religions, cults, and sects.
Most were about the Latter-day Saints (Mormons) and Jehovah's
Witnesses. There is a need to differentiate between formal church
teachings and the faith of individual believers whom people may
know personally, especially when doing so relates to "judging"
others.

Ethical issues are covered in chapter 7. A wide range of concerns confronts Christians as they make decisions in a rapidly changing world. Christians want freedom to live their own lives, but also want guidance from their churches. Church members want to know when they should conform to the group, and when they should stand alone. Questions on issues like these should be solved by going to the theological core of a question rather than settling for moralisms.

The final chapter deals with such matters as the relationship between church and state. What involvement should a congregation or churchwide office have on specific political issues? There are fewer questions coming to us in this area than on such concerns as worship or relationships within the parish. That may be simply because *The Lutheran* is a "church" publication. The lack of questions may indicate a reluctance on the part of Lutheran Christians to become fully engaged in the public world as Christians, although each person lives in that world every day. This chapter, therefore, includes a number of "Since You Didn't Ask" questions for readers of this book to respond to on their own or in discussion groups.

Use of the Book

This book is intended to stimulate thoughtful discussion in order that Christians might: (1) go deeper into their biblical and theological roots of faith, (2) appreciate the diversity within the members of the body of Christ, (3) celebrate unity in Christ, and (4) be equipped for mission and ministry in the public world. Now, the eight chapters do not provide definitive, absolute answers. How, then, might this book be used to accomplish its goals?

Some readers may prefer to read the book for their edification and enjoyment. We would hope they would not, however, read as an observer only, but as one personally engaged in the issues. There may well be personal and emotional, as well as intellectual, disagreement with the authors. That is to be expected, and may prove helpful. The authors, indeed the church itself, are no ultimate authority (only God is ultimate), although readers often add these words to their questions: "What does the church say about this matter?" The church is all of God's people bound together in Jesus Christ. The church is "we," not "they." This book, therefore, is but one part of a dialog to help the church be a faithful witness in contemporary society.

We encourage readers also to engage questions that do not personally involve them. We are never isolated Christians. If a friend or family member has a certain question, we are all called upon to help that person find clarity for action. In fact, thinking deeply about issues that do not passionately concern us teaches us to think objectively about matters that do.

While this book is appropriate for personal reading, it may prove most productive in a small group setting. Some people fear such encounters because "people always end up mad at each other." Indeed we, as authors, don't particularly enjoy receiving someone's words of wrath or judgment. Our goal is never to rile people up. Likewise, when this book is used in a group setting we trust the central objective will *not* be to stir things up. This book is not for spectators who want to sit and see a fight, but for participants who want to contribute to solving these issues.

Small group settings may include Sunday morning adult classes and adult forums, women's groups, men's groups, youth groups, Bible study groups, and discussion groups that meet in homes. If this book is used in an adult forum or other large gathering, be sure to divide the participants into smaller groups, perhaps six to eight people.

In arranging to discuss the material in these chapters, you can plan according to the time available and the wishes of your group. You might plan for eight sessions (one session per chapter) or 16 (two sessions per chapter). You may find that some topics will hold everyone's interest longer; spend more time on those if your calendar allows.

Ways to Encourage Group Discussion

How, then, might people with differing ideas and perspectives interact with this book? Most importantly, a safe learning environment must be set up. If people fear being judged or ridiculed or "out-argued," very few will participate. Once a safe environment of mutual respect is established, honest conflict—because of differences of opinion—can be welcomed.

This book can be an exercise in how to deal with conflict. In most cases, these questions and the conflict they represent (either within the reader or the reader's congregation) may provide ways to talk through issues before they become one's own. Such discussion might even forestall similar problems from arising later.

As the facilitator begins, he or she will help each person feel welcome and significant. One will need a comfortable setting and a convenient time. The group should be large enough to include a variety of opinions but small enough so nobody feels uncomfortable sharing. A broad range of ages and types of backgrounds is helpful as long as no one is given preferential treatment because of age, sex, or position. It's often helpful for people to "speak themselves present." Once someone gives one's name or tells of something that is going on in one's life at the time, that one is more likely to speak again. Most of us have been in a group where, reluctant to speak early on, we never feel able to "jump in" after things have gotten going.

There are many ways the questions and responses in these chapters can be approached. Here are two:

1) Read each question and its response. Then begin the discussion, using some of the helps given in the following pages.

2) While the others' books are closed, have someone read the question without the response. Talk together about how each of you would respond; then read the response in the book and continue the discussion. Chapter 8 has a number of open-ended questions; the group will develop their own responses for them.

If necessary, the leader can propose some "group rules," such as asking each person to speak from personal perspective using "I believe" or "I hold this opinion." This works better than presuming others hold a certain view, such as "Everyone thinks that . . ." or "You'll find when you get older that you believe as I do. . . ." Because we do not know how another feels or will think, such statements cut off a needed perspective and can lead quickly to arguments.

Human beings are subjective. Subjectivity itself is not a problem as long as it is acknowledged. I may have a certain bias because of my personal experience. It is helpful to acknowledge it as such and, if I know where that bias is coming from, perhaps even to share it. "I'm afraid of motorcycles and believe that helmets should be required . . . and I think that's because my step-brother and my cousin were killed in motorcycle accidents." Acknowledged biases can actually aid a group discussion.

Even though complete objectivity in human discussion is impossible, we *can* strive for clarity. A group can learn to be learners together. They can learn to keep the discussion environment safe for all, invite someone to speak whose views have not yet been expressed, and move a group back on track. Try asking, What is really being asked here? and What issues are included in the question to help guide discussion? A group can identify issues and even add subtleties and additional issues not expressed in the question. It is not helpful to assign a motive, e.g., "Well, it's obvious this person just has a grudge because he's . . ." or "All (racial, ethnic, church groups) think that way. . . ."

Even though questions often are worded What does the church say? or What should I do? a helpful discussion will ask the deeper questions behind the questions. If there is debate about extraneous noise during worship, the question is probably also about the nature of worship and the differences among us in our ability to deal with distraction. There are even deeper issues about the purpose of gathering for worship, about the nature of Christian community, and about the nature of the holy. If your discussion moves into those deeper issues, the book will have served its purpose.

Ministry and Mission Goals

The goal for use of this book is not to find the "right" answer nor to prove the authors right or wrong or good or bad, but to help the community where you are to grow. It is important to act courageously in mission in the world; Christians and the church need to take stands in order to be witnesses. Because the church's life together is always giving a message to the world, the church cannot decide not to decide.

The church, the people of God, in the place where you are is the curriculum of God. You are God's people in your time and place. This and all other printed material are resources. We trust this book will serve you well as you minister to one another.

There are other things you might want to consider. The group might want to pledge confidentiality to one another so that each feels free to express feelings and beliefs without fear of being quoted out of context later. (This may seem obvious, but explicit reminders often help because all of us have the tendency to forget.) As a safe learning environment is maintained, people may feel increasingly able to express their opinions. They may need to test the waters before jumping in and test out each other to see if their opinion is heard and respected. A good facilitator will frequently "gather" the thoughts expressed by saying them back to the group in brief summary form as a way of focusing where the group might yet go in the discussion. As the leader models this, others will not only listen to each other but actually hear and refer to what has been said, or ask another, "Would you say more about that? I find that an interesting view."

The Christian community that discusses issues has done only half the task. Learning is for mission. Our thinking clearly, discussing thoroughly, listening well, and growing in Christ are done so we will be able to minister well in daily life in the world. As a group continues to be together, we hope they bring back to each other their own dilemmas from the week and use their skill to deal with those questions of mission and ministry.

About the Writing of This Book

This book contains all the questions and responses printed during the first year of the "Since You Asked" column in *The Lutheran*.

What you often find here are slightly longer versions, reflecting the fact that, due to space, some editing was done before the columns were printed. In some chapters there are "Since You Answered" responses from readers, which both show how the authors were "heard" and add new dimensions not in the original column. In some chapters there is a "Since You Didn't Ask" section, indicating directions not yet taken and issues no one raised. Chapter 8 has a number of these, giving your group a chance to try its hand at our task. Your group might want to bring in additional "Since You Didn't Ask" questions and even send them to us for future columns.

Some people wonder if the letters we receive are real. Yes! We do not make any up. If we err, it is on the side of taking every reader seriously. Letters come from virtually all over the country, with no area represented more than any other. They are from urban, small town, and rural areas. They are from clergy, Associates in Ministry, and lay people. They appear to come from young adult, middle-aged, and retired people. They are typed or handwritten, lengthy or on postcards.

One cannot glean from the questions any statistical con-clusions about what issues are facing Lutherans in America today. This is a random sampling of issues from those who chose to write. We sometimes hear from people beyond the membership of the ELCA. Letters come from people in the Lutheran Church–Missouri Synod and members of other denominations who have read *The Lutheran* magazine, perhaps in a hospital waiting room, or who have received it through a friend or relative.

Some letters are short, others are many pages long, telling about the life situation, problems, and joys of the letter writer. We are often tempted to sit down and write letters back, but the volume of mail precludes that luxury. And that is not the purpose. We receive readers' questions and use them in a column for the enrichment of the church. It would be presumptuous of us to do personal one-on-one ministry through the mail. Christians listen and care for one another where they are, face-to-face, where they can put an arm on another's shoulder. We trust that you are doing that with people with whom you are called to minister in the place where you are. In particular we assume congregational members will exercise the responsibility of speaking directly to other members, pastors, church officers, and church staff members. Nowhere is this more true than when there is disagreement and conflict.

Our concerns when invited to write the column were these: (1) It should not be a "let's watch them fight" column. (2) It should not be a humor column. (There is another place for that; we would never intentionally ridicule a writer). (3) We wanted to deal with the core of the gospel; each question should concern an element basic to the faith.

The column is not simply a place for information and opinion. We consider ourselves to have a special ministry in the church—a ministry of education. We trust this book will be received as it is intended.

About the Authors

Some have asked how we write. Our editor sends us all letters received by *The Lutheran* concerning our column, without screening or selecting. We read all the letters as we receive them and decide which ones might have general reader interest. We try to balance the types of questions, then we decide which of us will work on a certain question. Next we discuss each question together (just as you might be doing in your home or group with this book). Sometimes we consult with clergy, Associates in Ministry, and laity here and around the church. We then write independently on our selected questions and submit them to one another for editing. This is essentially the same process we have used in writing this book.

All of our responses have been published. We have received *no* letters assuming one or the other wrote a certain answer because we were male or female. In fact, readers might be quite surprised to know which of us writes which response. Our theological positions are similar yet different enough to enrich and complement the other. We gain from doing the column together because we share insights that neither or us alone would have. We listen to each other and try to include the views of the other in our response. On occasion we disagree, although not on basic matters of faith.

Although we have seen an interesting assortment of ways letters are addressed (including some to "Norman"), for the most part, even those who have trouble with the ordination of women give us their respect in addressing us. The church's reception of a couple in ministry serving together in this way has been a hopeful sign of ministry of men and women in the church at large.

We write from our perspective, which is partially shaped by our life experience. Cumulatively we have been in the public ministry of the church for over 50 years, serving in five of the nine regions of the ELCA, in its three predecessor bodies, in inner-city, suburban, and rural communities. We have been enriched by the diverse people among whom it has been a privilege and a blessing to serve. We have been married for 27 years and have three sons—Mark, 26, Joel, 22, and Kirk, 20—who are all engaged in their own creative work. We appreciate their encouragement of our ministries. Norma is an associate professor in the Division of Ministry at Wartburg Theological Seminary in Dubuque, Iowa. Burton is pastor of Grace Lutheran Church in East Dubuque, Illinois. (Although we work in two different states, those two positions are only four miles apart.) Our appreciation goes to colleagues at Wartburg and parishioners at Grace Lutheran; their friendship and support is an ongoing encouragement.

We wish to give our appreciation to the Reverend David Miller, Senior Features Editor of *The Lutheran*, who invited us to write the column and who faithfully sends us letters received and edits our material. We also appreciate Editor Edgar Trexler and the staff at *The Lutheran*. This is a partnership with them as well. We particularly appreciate working with Irene Getz and John Hanka, the editors of this book, and the entire staff at Augsburg Fortress, who encouraged us to do this book and who published it for your use.

1

Differences over Ways of Worship

It all begins with worship, as we are baptized into Jesus Christ. Worship is the core of our existence, for in the context of our worship we are knit together in Christ. The body of Christ, the people of God, are nourished and nurtured by the reading and hearing of God's Word and the receiving of Christ's body and blood. Each Lord's Day we gather for nourishment and then scatter to serve.

Questions about worship cover even the preparations prior to the service itself, for instance, the choice of flowers to put on the altar.

QUESTION   May only live flowers be placed on the altar? For those living in the North, purchasing winter flowers is expensive. Beautiful silk and plastic flowers look so real it's hard to tell the difference.

RESPONSE   In worship, the symbol of growth is as significant as beauty. Using flowers from our yards or roadsides is fitting and avoids great expense. Churches in regions with cold winter seasons use dried arrangements such as wheat, the dormant beauty of which promises new growth to come. Potted plants serve well because they add signs of life and growth. Artificial flowers simply cannot do that. Our care about such matters praises God. But do not be too burdened by what we place on the altar. Focus on what God places there—the eucharistic meal that enables us to grow so that people can tell there's a difference in our lives.

■ Careful attention to the elements of our worship is, of course, fitting. Yet it seems sometimes that more attention is paid to what *we* do in worship than to what *God* is giving to us. There is a curious sadness that on many Sundays care is taken to provide the supporting elements—flowers, paraments, banners, vestments, and music—while the central gift of Christ's own body and blood in the bread and wine are not provided.

Moving from preparations into worship itself, we immediately encounter questions about the ways we enter the service. The processional cross, a powerful visual element, evoked one question.

QUESTION   Is the processional cross used at all times or just for festivals?

RESPONSE   When there is a procession, it is always appropriate to include a processional cross. The procession does visually what the invocation and greeting do verbally: it focuses attention on Jesus' death and resurrection as the center of worship. Not only does a procession lead us into worship, but we also follow the cross out to the narthex, where we leave the church building and go into the world.

Of course processions, like vestments, are not necessary to celebrate Holy Communion. Some churches have a procession every Sunday. They are never simply parades. The inclusion and order of a procession, like the worship service itself, gives a message about our movement to God, then into the world.

■ Readers move toward the heart of worship life and find a key segment distressing: the greeting of peace. This most ancient custom, greeting one another with a holy kiss, the kiss of peace, has been so long unused by Western Christians that it appears to many—if not most—as disruptive. Many come to worship for comfort and security, expecting to find it in the familiar and customary. Many view worship as a collective activity of individuals, rather than as the communal activity of members of the one body of Christ.

QUESTION I recently read a syndicated columnist commenting on an informal worship survey conducted by *The Lutheran* (March 16, 1988, pp. 10-12). He wrote that one respondent mockingly described passing the peace as "peace where there is no peace." A number of those responding to the survey found the peace— with its aisle-hopping and emotional hugging and kissing—to be "fomenting mayhem." The major objection of those polled: The practice was a jarring intrusion to the mood of serious worship. What do you think?

RESPONSE In the same survey, people also said the greeting felt phony. The greeting of peace certainly does jar older styles and expectations of worship. Any worship action that is new to us feels—and is—awkward at first. When the peace was introduced in a Detroit congregation in the 1960s, a white man refused to greet his nearest neighbor, a black woman. After some discussion and reflection, his attitude changed and the full meaning of peace—reconciliation—was attained. That Detroit congregation learned the value of the greeting of peace. Once they learned it, they never stopped using it in their weekly Eucharist.

Peace is not simply to be equated with being quiet, nor is serious worship always solemn, nor is it hypocritical to share the peace when we do not feel like it. Hypocrisy is pretending so that people will think well of us. The peace we share is not our internal feelings, but the peace—reconciliation with God—

given by Christ. Sharing the peace is an act of love to encourage others. There are many for whom the "holy hug," accompanied by the word of God's peace, has been the way they knew once more that they were loved, forgiven, and cherished by God.

■ Nowhere is our worship together more intimate than at the table of the Lord. Jesus has instituted this supper in order to nourish us as the community of the redeemed. When diverse people gather and break bread together, differences are bound to surface. This is true even of the manner by which the elements are received.

QUESTION Some members of our congregation absolutely detest our new minister's insistence that we receive the communion bread in our hands. Why can't each person choose how he or she wishes to receive the bread, either in the new way or in the centuries-old, traditional way: on the tongue?

RESPONSE You express strong feelings! Are they rooted in basic convictions of the faith? Or are they reactions to your new pastor? Are you simply resisting change? Worship scholar Luther Reed notes that receiving the bread in one's hand "is the earliest form of reception, to which Tertullian and Cyril of Jerusalem both testify." The "new" way you describe is more ancient than the "traditional" procedure that some insist upon. The church began placing the consecrated bread directly in the mouth in medieval times to prevent people from taking it home to use as a magical charm.

It is unseemly for either you or your pastor to insist upon either procedure. Such a spirit borders on the lovelessness Paul warned the Corinthian Christians about when they failed to discern the body of Christ, the church. Holy Communion is a communal experience that intimately links the whole Christian community. It is a resource that enables us to care for each other.

Pray for God's guidance, approach your pastor, and pray together. Seek the core meaning and power of the Lord's Supper through study and prayer as a congregation. A worship committee could lead you in this study, searching the Scriptures, learning about the history of communion practices, and focusing on the purpose and meaning of the Lord's Supper. Draw upon the resources of the ELCA Division for Congregational Life or a seminary. Seek consensus based on prayerful study, rather than a majority vote. Serious, open searching will give you a hunger and thirst to receive frequently the rich gift of Christ's body and blood.

■ Not only the manner of reception, but the elements themselves, can become points of controversy. While no Lutheran would consider substituting other elements such as coffee or soda for the fruit of the vine, Lutherans have in some instances used grape juice rather than wine. This was the case raised by one reader.

QUESTION   What is the Evangelical Lutheran Church in America's position on wine versus grape juice for distribution at communion?

RESPONSE   The ELCA has not spoken to this issue yet, but wine is the element Jesus used. The use of grape juice was adopted in the 1800s because some churches did not approve of any alcoholic beverage, including wine. They took advantage of the newly discovered process of pasteurization, which stops the natural fermentation that ordinarily turns all fruit juices into wines or vinegars.

Some congregations encourage recovering alcoholics to receive the bread alone, since each element conveys the whole of Christ. Others have a second cup or small glasses filled with grape juice. When we do this openly, it reminds us all that no problem need hinder our life together in Christ. Visiting clergy need to be informed of the congregation's procedure. All who come to the table hear and receive the blessing, "The body and blood of our Lord Jesus Christ strengthen you and keep you in his grace."

Since You Answered

Two readers expressed their opinion that this practice was in disagreement with confessional positions. Certainly if someone insisted that our churches could not use wine, indeed must not use wine, we would consider it necessary to insist that wine be used. But the word wine is nowhere explicitly used in any of the accounts of the institution of the Lord's Supper. When Jesus did speak of the contents of the cup, it was as "the fruit of the vine." To be sure, it may be assumed that the cup contained wine, given the difficulty of keeping the fruit of the vine from fermenting naturally, and the Passover practice of using wine. It is also true that some alcoholics simply touch the cup to their lips without drinking. Nevertheless, it seems to border upon legalism to require that the vine's fruit be fermented.

■ Points of strain arise in the very singing of our hymns. There is a feeling that unless worship fits our own custom and preferences, it is not right.

QUESTION Why do some church organists improvise so much that hymns are unsingable? Shouldn't the organ play an assisting role to enhance the singing?

RESPONSE There is a tension between the desire of church musicians to use their gifts to provide greater variety and interest in worship, and the desire of people to sing easily the hymns they know and love. Singing is not competition. The organ should not impede the congregational singing. Hymns are the people's songs.

But as singing together expresses unity, so diversity in gifts also is important. In addition to special choral and instrumental music, certain verses of hymns can be times for the congregation to listen and receive from musicians their joy in the gospel. Such variations in accompaniment can be noted in the bulletin so that people understand what is happening. Organists and choirs primarily perform the important work of supporting congregations as they worship in song.

■ Lutheran worship at its best lives in the flow of the church year and brings to remembrance the life of Christ and the Spirit's presence in the church. As Lutherans have begun to restore much of their liturgical heritage (much of which had been discounted in overreaction to some Roman Catholic abuses), these restorations have been unsettling to members who were raised with different views. This is particularly true of the practice of marking worshipers' foreheads with ashes on Ash Wednesday.

QUESTION At Ash Wednesday services, our pastor offered the imposition of ashes for those who desired them. I was taught we did not need ashes on our foreheads to remind us we are all dust and to dust we shall return. Has this teaching changed?

RESPONSE Ash Wednesday received its name from the imposition of ashes, which usually occurred at a morning service on the first day of Lent. True, ashes are not necessary to remind us we are dust, but they can help. Some people are self-conscious about others seeing them with an ashmark on their foreheads. This self-consciousness helps them remember all day long their human frailty.

The ashes are made by burning the palm fronds from the previous year's Palm Sunday celebration. They can remind us all—whether we receive them or not—that God gave us the crucified and risen Jesus so that our praises will not wither at the foot of the cross.

Many recall Jesus' counsel that we are not to disfigure our faces as the hypocrites do in order to be admired. If we receive ashes to be patted on the back, this would be wrong. In our day, however, admiration for wearing ashes is unlikely, since our society tries to deny death and does not encourage open expression of faith. Ashes today can be an unsettling warning of human mortality.

Since most Lutheran Ash Wednesday services are held in the evening, we do not receive the full reminder that we could have. When ashes are imposed at evening services, some congregations have placed the baptismal font at the door and encourage people to wash the ashes with water as a reminder of their Baptism. In this way, worshipers are reminded that they die with Christ and rise with Christ each day.

■ Another service that has been restored by Lutherans is the Easter vigil, a liturgy including the original candle-lighting service (which the Christmas candle-lighting service echoes) and celebrates the great conclusion of the Lenten season. Inquiries sometimes center on specific aspects of the "new" orders, as in this case.

QUESTION Our church has added a Saturday night service in Holy Week—the Vigil of Easter. Is this common in Lutheran churches now? This service describes the Fall as the "necessary sin of Adam" and a "happy fault." Where does this language come from? Can it be justified?

RESPONSE The Easter vigil is, perhaps, the oldest festival service in the Christian church. It is a "watch" for the risen Christ. In the early church, the service began at sundown on Saturday—

the time Sunday began in Jewish tradition—and climaxed at sunrise. It included the Baptism of adults who had been instructed for the 40 days of Lent and concluded with the Lord's Supper.

The vigil, as outlined in the *Lutheran Book of Worship Minister's Desk Edition*, uses a series of prayers and Scripture readings to unfold the meaning of the redemption God has worked for us through Christ's death and resurrection.

While considerably shorter than the service held by early Christians, the *LBW* version retains its central themes. It focuses especially on Baptism, stressing our union in Baptism with Christ's death and resurrection. Not every congregation is using this service, but those who do find that it enlivens their faith.

The language you mentioned about the Fall is part of the vigil's Easter proclamation. It is poetic, exuberant, and comes from a pre–sixth-century Christian liturgy. The words are intended to accent the depth of God's love. It is one way of saying that without the Fall we would not have seen the depth of God's love. We would not know Jesus died for us.

■ Toward the end of the church year comes a cluster of days that seem difficult to separate. Some wonder how they can understand the uniqueness of those days.

QUESTION What is the difference between Halloween, All Saints' Day, and All Souls' Day?

RESPONSE According to *The Oxford Dictionary of the Christian Church,* All Saints' Day is "The feast, kept in the West on Nov. 1 to celebrate all the Christian saints, known and unknown," and All Souls' Day is "The commemoration on Nov. 2 of the souls of the faithful departed."

The *Lutheran Book of Worship* includes only November 1, All Saints' Day, in its list of "Lesser Festivals and Commemorations." The *LBW Manual on the Liturgy* notes that day as an "appropriate time to remember members of the congregation who have died during the past year" but urges also a broader remembrance of "all the saints of God."

Halloween, October 31, is historically the hallowed or holy eve of All Saints' Day. In the United States today there are secular meanings and activities associated with Halloween. Children don costumes and masquerade as imaginary characters, going from house to house saying, "Trick or treat." In recent years Halloween has sometimes turned to tragedy through poisoned candy. Congregations and communities appropriately seek safe ways for children to enjoy this cultural holiday.

October 31, of course, is also Reformation Day, the day Martin Luther posted his 95 theses on the door of the Castle Church in Wittenberg. The posting of this list of grievances against the Roman Catholicism of that day is an event of great historical and theological significance, particularly for Lutherans.

■ Questions regarding cremation frequently cross our desk, apparently sent by readers who missed our earlier response to that issue.

QUESTION Is there anything in the Bible about cremation?

RESPONSE Scripture says nothing about cremation. Early Christians chose the burial of Jesus as their model. Since some people cremated to mock the promise of the resurrection, Christians avoided it.

Lutherans since the early 1900s have permitted cremation but have recommended burial. Interment reminds us we are buried with Christ and rise to newness of life. The preaching of the gospel and the sharing of the Lord's Supper are the best ways of remembering the victory of the resurrection, whether burial or cremation is used.

■ The most solemn and awesome moment for each of us is the time we face death, our own above all, but also the death of those we love dearly. Two more questions raise concerns about worship on such occasions.

QUESTION My husband died over 10 years ago. We had talked of death when both of us were hale and hearty. We planned his funeral together before he died. We first had visitation at the funeral home, then burial, then a memorial service and fellowship at the church. Now I want my funeral the same way and our children think it is a good arrangement. Does the church have anything to say concerning this?

RESPONSE You and your husband displayed a beautiful Christian faith by discussing your deaths and funeral arrangements while you were still quite healthy. What is important in every Christian's funeral is a clear witness to Christ's victory over death and the certainty of our resurrection.

The way you chose is certainly acceptable, but there is something to be said for bringing the bodies of God's children to church. There the casket would pass the baptismal font, and we would be reminded that we have died with Christ and are risen with Christ in Baptism. There the paschal candle, a symbol of the risen Christ's presence, can remind us of God's astonishing victory over death. There the Supper of the Lord can be shared to comfort and encourage us as we proclaim the Lord's death till he returns. These are powerful gifts that are good to claim in this most awesome time of our lives.

But we cannot make requirements of these gifts, and a conversation now with your pastor should help you work together so that your funeral proclaims Christ's victory, gives comfort to your loved ones, and gives strength to others in the community of the risen Christ. There are a variety of options open to you. Discuss them with your pastor so your funeral will reflect your desires.

QUESTION   Why does the Lutheran church almost ignore memories of and memorial services for our beloved deceased? Why do clergy have trouble speaking about the hereafter, death, and eternal life?

RESPONSE   You have two questions here. In response to your first one, it is unfortunate that some congregations do not celebrate the lives of the saints. *The Lutheran Book of Worship* offers rich opportunities to remember the faithful who have died. The "Commemorations" section in *LBW* (pp. 36ff.) provides prayers and lessons that can be used to celebrate not only the lives of the saints listed on the hymnal's calendar (pp. 10ff.), but also some nonfamous saints, relatives, and friends we remember and love long after their deaths.

Many congregations use the Sunday nearest All Saints' Day on November 1 to remember by name members who have died in the past year. Congregations might include in their histories biographies and photos of deceased members. In one congregation, a family used memorial funds to sponsor an annual service of performing arts. Others, of course, honor their beloved's memory by giving to mission projects that were treasured by the deceased.

In response to your second question, clergy are equipped with pastoral care skills to use in times of death, loss, and grief. Still, each must struggle with their own fear and even denial of death. The *Occasional Services* book has services for times of "impending death" and "acceptance of inevitable death." One might note fewer references to the hereafter in sermons in recent years, but most pastors speak a great deal about salvation connecting the reality of new life in Christ on earth with eternal life in heaven. Christians are strengthened in their hope of heaven by hearing it spoken from the pulpit and in daily conversation. We are rightly reluctant to describe the details of the hereafter or to preach about heaven to the neglect of Christian mission now on earth, but all ages need to hear that Christ's resurrection victory is good news for us now and eternally.

■ It becomes clear in question after question that lay members view some of the changes in their worship life as intrusions foisted on them by their pastors. Much conflict revolves around the relationships between pastors, staffs, and people, as the next chapter shows.

2

Conflict over Leadership Roles

The Christian community God creates is entirely human. It is not without reason that the Third Article of the Apostles' Creed links the Holy Spirit, the church, and the forgiveness of sins. It is through the people of God that God conveys life-giving mercy. To nourish and nurture each other and to enable outreach, the church receives with joy the Spirit's gifts of brothers and sisters who lead in the public ministry of the church.

But the presence of those who exercise public service, formally representing the whole people of God, gives rise to tensions as well as blessings. This chapter focuses on the relationships between congregational members and those who serve the church in public capacities.

Our first question does not initially appear to speak to issues of public ministry, but it provides a basic perspective.

QUESTION Could you explain the religious significance and responsibilities of godparents or sponsors at a Lutheran Baptism? Are they required to be Lutherans, or is it just a recommendation?

RESPONSE With the renewed emphasis on Baptism, your question takes on important meaning. The sponsors present each candidate; the entire congregation confesses the faith and welcomes the new sisters and brothers into God's family as members of the body of Christ. The sponsors are caring Christians who are a sign and one means for the entire congregation to carry out their responsibility of nurturing these new Christians, whether they be infants or adults. The sponsors, therefore, in most cases should be Lutheran.

In a time of mobile and changing families, sponsors are not now chosen primarily to honor certain relatives or to raise a child in case of the death of the parents. Sponsors help people celebrate their baptismal day each year—not just until confirmation, but throughout their lives. We appreciate such Christians who, even when the family moves across the country, form a link from congregation to congregation and who continue to love, pray for, write to, and diligently help the children they sponsor grow in the faith into which they were baptized.

■ Christian Baptism is impossible without Christian community. People don't baptize themselves. Sponsors exercise a limited public ministry, not instead of, but in behalf of the larger body of Christians. Everyone is responsible for every other baptized Christian, but some have been given more specific responsibility than others. That this ministry and responsibility belongs to all of us does not mean that this ministry is not exercised in particular ways by those whom the church designates for those tasks.

Sponsors receive specific charges, limited to designated individuals. Those who exercise public ministry to congregations, synods, regions, and the Evangelical Lutheran Church in America as a whole offer different services and have differing responsibilities. In the Evangelical Lutheran Church in America, the public ministers of the church are now called clergy and Associates in Ministry. Most questions we received dealt with the ministry of pastors and people in congregations.

One question focused on a key dilemma: What is the task of the people and what is the task of the pastor?

QUESTION Our pastor insists that church members are ministers and should make a large majority of the evangelism calls. While our members do make their share, the pastor very infrequently calls on prospective members and is very reluctant to respond to members' requests to make home visits. How should this problem be handled?

RESPONSE You might invite pastor and lay members to meet regularly to talk about the calls each has made. Pastors should call on prospective members and on congregation members, not just in time of crisis or when asked, but as an ongoing ministry. And yes, congregation members are ministers and also should share their faith with others in the community. Outreach ministry is a shared task.

The goal of equipping the laity is not that pastors "work themselves out of a job." As more people speak about the meaning of the gospel in this complex world and discover the needs of people in the community, ministry opportunities for clergy and laity are multiplied. Discussing the questions and concerns encountered in making calls may increase the interest, listening skills, and theological insight of your pastor and church members.

■ Baptism gives every member of the body of Christ the commission to witness to Jesus Christ. All have responsibility for sharing him with those who don't know him, and for encouraging, exhorting, admonishing, teaching, comforting, and upbuilding one another in the faith. It is the pastor's task to "equip the saints" for this ministry. But this is not done simply by administration or instruction; it also requires pastoral leadership to participate in these efforts side-by-side with the people. This can provide the people with encouragement and examples, and can deepen the pastor's understanding of the members' needs and problems.

Another questioner widened the focus: "Can you explain to us just what a congregation should expect a pastor to do and not to do?" The fact that the inquirer did not ask, Just what should a congregation's membership be expected to do? illuminates the issue. Questions of ministry need to be addressed in the larger framework of the work of the whole people of God, together as people, pastors, and Associates in Ministry.

One inquirer was concerned about weaknesses in a pastor's abilities to work with the youth, in particular, a confirmation class.

QUESTION Our pastor gives fine sermons and is well liked by adults. What can be done to help him make confirmation class more interesting?

RESPONSE Some pastors find ministry with adults easier than ministry with young people. Pastors struggle with discipline and disinterest and soon dread class as much as the students. But turning things around may not necessarily take a miracle.

Students say: "What's most important to us is what's going on in our own lives." They learn from a pastor who is interested in them. It may help if ways can be developed for the pastor and young people to interact with each other outside of class.

Some congregations are beginning to approach confirmation as an ongoing pastoral and educational ministry, and are not trying to instill all Christian doctrine in the junior high years. They involve families, lay catechists, and mentors over many years so that the young Christians are continually relating their faith to their changing lives.

The broader church offers continuing education on developmental stages of children and youth and a variety of educational methods. Using such resources, available through Augsburg Fortress, Publishers and the Division for Congregational Life of the Evangelical Lutheran Church in America, students and teachers might find each other more interesting and enjoyable.

■ In a real sense, the discussion of confirmation is a continuation of the first question in this section about Baptism and sponsors. When confirmation is seen as affirmation of our Baptism, it becomes clear that the task of instruction is shared by the family, sponsors, congregation, church staff, pastor, and the wider church. The *Small Catechism* was intended by Martin Luther to be taught, discussed, and prayed in the home. While pastors bear primary responsibility for the teaching ministry of the church, they cannot, they should not, exercise this work alone.

Some readers are puzzled by certain practices of their pastors, such as how often they take the Lord's Supper.

QUESTION Our pastor, who serves several congregations, does not partake of communion. If he expects his parishoners to take communion, shouldn't he?

RESPONSE You do not say if he does not commune at each church, or if he does not commune at all. Holy Communion is a gift, not a duty. Some fear "taking it too often" might diminish its meaning, while others commune weekly. Martin Luther advocated daily communion.

The Lord's Supper is a communal meal. If a pastor serves more than one congregation, it is appropriate to receive the elements with each congregation. Not only is this a sign that we need to receive the body of Christ, but that we each are part of the body of Christ.

If you never see your pastor commune, ask him why. Perhaps your pastor has a spiritual problem and could use your care and encouragement.

■ When problems arise, it is always best to speak directly to the person involved, be it a pastor, a member of the staff, a council member, or another member of the congregation. Some find this most difficult to do when it is the pastor with whom they have a problem. For this reason, many congregations have committees that work with pastors and staff members concerning problems that arise. Where such committees exist it is good to use them, and where they do not exist it may be good to form them.

Readers have also shared questions that have long puzzled them, such as the following inquiry about clerical collars.

QUESTION I am curious about the clerical collar Lutheran ministers wear. I noticed in your photo in *The Lutheran* that one of you has a full, white collar and the other a collar with a square of white in front only. Why? Also, I thought the white collar on the black shirt symbolized the light of Christ emerging from the darkness. But pastors wear different colors such as red or light blue.

RESPONSE Religious practices wind their way through history in intriguing ways. In this case it is almost impossible to trace exact historical roots. Most authorities agree the "clerical collar" was the street garb of the Middle Ages. The different styles you note simply display the diversity in clerical apparel today.

It seems strange that an ordinary medieval collar should be a symbol in modern times, but it is. In this complex culture filled with changing, competing symbols, the clerical collar still identifies purpose, availability, and confidentiality both among parishioners and in the community at large. It says one may expect from the person wearing it a clear word of gospel on behalf of the church. It is also a reminder to the pastors who wear it of the responsibility they carry.

Clergy vary widely in how frequently they wear a collar. One does not take up or discharge the role and responsibility of pastor by putting on or taking off a collar. There is no official Lutheran position on the matter. But for the sake of ministry a pastor should choose clothing for ready identification by those he or she serves. (The Council of Trent, 1545–63, said "clerics always wear a dress conformable to their order, that by the propriety of their outward apparel they may show forth the inward uprightness of their morals.")

In recent years clerical shirts and blouses have become available in a range of colors. You are correct that black and white have symbolized light and darkness. But historically the cleric's garb may have been black for practical, not symbolic reasons. One needs to be careful in this racist world about equating black with darkness and sin, and white with light and purity. It may contribute to the ongoing oppression of one race by another.

■ Among the most anguishing questions are those that concern immoral behavior by pastors.

QUESTION Does the church condone the behavior of its pastors who use their position to seduce parishioners and carry on adulterous affairs?

RESPONSE No, the church does not condone adultery by pastors or by members. Clergy have a position of trust as counselors, confessors, and teachers, and they must not become involved with parishioners in physically or emotionally inappropriate ways.

This is a serious matter and a critical charge. If true, it must be stopped. If false, the pastor's and member's reputation must be protected. Speak directly to the pastor and member first. If there is proof and they reject correction, bring it to the attention of your congregation's leadership, but do not speak to other members about it. Many congregations have a pastor-parish committee, a staff committee, or their equivalent to deal with questions of clergy performance and conduct.

If this does not bring results, take your concern to your synod bishop, again in confidence. The bylaws of the Evangelical Lutheran Church in America outline approved procedures to deal with this and other problems relating to clergy conduct and competence. Pastors, as well as parishioners, can be brought to repentance in Christ and helped to change their lives.

Since You Answered

One reader responded that this answer sounded good, but the procedure as outlined above was not being used where he lived. "When we look up from the magazine, we see churches where pastors engage in sexual promiscuity. . . . Perhaps things aren't as rampant where you live. The church of which you write doesn't appear to exist in many parts of this country."

Sexual promiscuity is a problem in every part of the country. If someone sees churches where this is the case, it is absolutely necessary for him or her to take direct action. As the response stressed, we need to speak directly to the people involved. We must be certain we are not dealing with rumor. If there is no response and our information is accurate, we must bring the situation to the attention of responsible church leadership. Anything less fails to fulfill one's responsibility to correct the erring sister or brother, and that person then becomes part of the problem.

■ In the 1700s Muhlenberg, concerned about the low wages of preachers, wrote, "It is easier to be a cowherd in Germany than a preacher in America." Some congregations provided parsonages with several acres of land on which the pastor could raise food and keep stock for the family, but this was unusual. Others brought goods to the pastor, though no salary. It would appear that someone writing to *The Lutheran* in the 1700s might have expressed concern that pastors were receiving too much for too little, as in the next question. Many congregations were unwilling at that time to bind themselves to any specified amount and even such commitments held, as a rule, for only a year!

QUESTION Our pastor's salary plus housing allowance and benefits seem like an incredible amount of money for a woman who works only on Sunday mornings and leads a Bible study and a few meetings a week. Why do we pay her that sum, especially when her husband has a good job and since clergy don't pay taxes? Should those who are called to serve get rich off their congregations?

RESPONSE Clergy work all week and pay federal, state, and self-employment social security taxes on their salary, though their housing allowances are exempt from taxation by the federal and some state governments. Congregations should pay their pastors according to synod guidelines on the basis of years of service, not in relation to the spouse's job. Women clergy face a problem similar to other women in the congregation—not being taken seriously. We need to see them as contributing, responsible adults. No Christian is called to become rich at the expense of others. The questions you pose concerning worth and fairness can erode a relationship. If you do not know what your pastor does, you need to ask her.

■ There was a time when seminary students were supported entirely while studying at the churches' seminaries in preparation for pastoral ministry. Now many students graduate with a debt load due to the cost of college and seminary education. The education of pastors, both in preparation for ordination and throughout their pastoral service, is essential to the work of the church.

Doctors, dentists, nurses, lawyers, business people, farmers, technicians, and many others regularly participate in continuing education in order to be more effective and well informed. Continuing education is equally important for the pastors of the church. But some members, whose life does not include regular updating of their own education, have difficulties understanding this. Therefore, they wonder, as does the following correspondent, why their pastors should have their studies underwritten by the congregation.

QUESTION Should a congregation pay for their pastor's doctorate? I always thought that pastors should pay for their own educational advancement.

RESPONSE Few pastors pursue a Ph.D., a degree that involves heavy personal expense in time and money. More pastors in recent years are studying for a Doctor of Ministry, a professional degree enhancing pastoral expertise, which one pursues while engaged in pastoral ministry. While responsibility for the work, time, and finances belongs to the person pursuing the degree, some pastors, quite appropriately, use the continuing education time and funds provided by their congregations for this purpose.

All pastors are expected to engage regularly in continuing education. Some attend a variety of conferences and seminars; others prefer to focus their work through a degree program. Congregations are strongly urged or required, often by synod guidelines, to budget time (not considered vacation) and funds (pastors contribute personal funds as well), not simply for personal "advancement," but so that the congregation's ministry will be enhanced through their pastor's growth.

Congregations, through synods and the churchwide body, also contribute to the education of ministers by supporting seminaries and seminarians. The educational ministry of a congregation includes lifelong learning for lay people and clergy alike.

■ While most questions concerned pastoral leadership, one was interested in the work of the deaconesses of the church.

QUESTION What has become of deaconesses? Where are they? How many are left? Do they still wear a habit?

RESPONSE There are several Lutheran deaconess communities in this country. The Lutheran Deaconess Association, an inter-Lutheran community (1304 LaPorte Ave., Valparaiso IN 46383) has consecrated over 600 deaconesses in the past 70 years, 300 of whom are involved in service today. You may see them serving and living out their diaconal commitment almost anywhere, in a parish, in an inner-city justice program, on a college campus, or in a medical center. Deaconesses offer workshops for laity, emphasizing the diaconal work of the church in daily vocation. Many serve in ELCA congregations and institutions; many serve in other church-related ministries. Some deaconesses serve in a variety of human service occupations in the public world. Although navy blue is traditional dress, they usually wear regular street clothes and their deaconess pin.

The Deaconess Community of the ELCA (801 Merion Square Rd., Gladwyne PA 19035–1599) has 125 in its community of "set apart" deaconesses. They serve in congregations, church-related agencies, and institutions in the United States and Canada. They may choose to wear the official garb: a black dress with white collar for formal occasions and a grey dress for informal. While still active in traditional roles of Christian education and youth ministry, today a deaconess sister may be found serving in a hospital with abandoned babies or coordinating community services for the aged.

Both of the above communities actively recruit women of all ages. The Deaconess Community also sponsors a one-year volunteer program of diaconal associates.

The Lutheran Deaconess Motherhouse (4535 N. 92nd, Milwaukee WI 53225), in continuous existence since 1849, has consecrated about 200 deaconesses. After a lifetime of service in hospital-related professions, social work, and administration, most of them are now retired. They do not wear official garb but do have a deaconess pin.

In addition to those three, there are several other deaconess communities, including the Lutheran Deaconess Association of Chicago and the Concordia Community in River Forest, Illinois, the latter serving the Lutheran Church–Missouri Synod.

Lutheran deaconesses in the United States are part of an ecumenical global deaconess movement, Diakonia, which includes thousands of deaconesses from the Americas and the

Caribbean, Europe, Asia, and Africa. Deaconess ministry remains a vital opportunity both for service and for community.

Since You Answered

This question and response stimulated a number of responses. Apparently the ministry of deaconesses is of keen interest in the church. One writer, a nurse educated at a Lutheran college, wrote, "I know God has a calling for me." She had found the information about this ministry opportunity valuable and encouraging.

One reader wondered, "How will I recognize the pin, which will probably be my only clue if I meet a deaconess?"

The pin worn by the Valparaiso-based deaconess association is a cross-shaped pin with the Greek Chi-Rho symbol and a basin. These are symbols of the service rendered by those who waited on tables, service raised to new meaning by Jesus himself when he washed the feet of the disciples on Maundy Thursday. The pin of the Gladwyne-based community symbolizes the three motherhouses in Philadelphia, Baltimore, and Omaha, which merged to form their present community. Deaconesses of the Milwaukee-based community wear, from a bar or chain, a two-inch, silver cross with the date of one's consecration on one side and a favorite Bible verse on the other. The reader may wish to write the three communities that serve the Evangelical Lutheran Church in America at the addresses listed in the above answer and invite a speaker or request further information directly from them.

A young man inquired, "I do not feel I have a calling to the ordained ministry, but I do believe I may have a calling to service through the diaconate. Where can I get information about the permanent diaconate in the Evangelical Lutheran Church in America?"

The current yearbook of the Evangelical Lutheran Church in America lists deaconesses and deacons who were rostered in the Association of Evangelical Lutheran Churches, a predecessor church body, and who are now rostered in the Evangelical Lutheran Church in America. Further information about the avenue of service they are providing may be obtained by writing any of the people listed on that roster.

Since You Didn't Ask

The preceding response to our discussion of diaconal ministry touched on an issue that, surprisingly, was not raised by any questioner.

QUESTION   The roster in the current yearbook of the Evangelical Lutheran Church in America lists not only the ordained ministers (or clergy) but also a category new to us: Associates in Ministry. Who are "Associates in Ministry" and how did they come to be listed? Will they be a permanent category?

RESPONSE   Associates in Ministry are people who serve the Evangelical Lutheran Church in America in salaried public capacities other than the ministry of Word and Sacrament. These include service as educators (both Christian day school teachers and parish educators), administrators, social workers, secretaries, musicians, and as deaconesses and deacons. Their names came from the rosters of the Evangelical Lutheran Church in America's predecessor church bodies. New Associates in Ministry are being received regularly by a process under the authority of the Evangelical Lutheran Church in America through the Division for Ministry. Generally, Associates in Ministry have received theological education and are expected to participate in continuing theological education as they serve. Usually they are salaried by various institutions within the Evangelical Lutheran Church in America, although in some instances they serve outside the formal church structure but respond to their church's oversight.

In many ways these public ministries continue the ministry of Jesus as he described it, quoting Isaiah: "The Spirit of the

Lord is upon me, for the Lord has anointed me to preach good news to the poor. The Lord has sent me to proclaim release to the captives and recovering of sight to the blind, to set at liberty those who are oppressed, to proclaim the acceptable year of the Lord'' (Luke 4:18-19).

The place of Associates in Ministry in the Evangelical Lutheran Church in America is under study, led by the Task Force on the Study of Ministry.

■ As the people of God work together with pastors and Associates in Ministry, they encounter problems having to do with specific programs and procedures. These are taken up in the following chapter.

3

Life Together
in the Congregation

By the power of the Spirit we have been given to each other as gifts, yet people often have problems with one another. The church is a place where forgiven sinners live together, confessing that they are the body of Christ. The church is historic and global, so no one congregation is the entire church. Yet the church is both universal and particular. Each congregation is the church. And, whether rural or urban, large or small, the problems of life together in one congregation are often similar to those in other congregations as well. We ought not be surprised. We are God's gifts to each other, but the difficulties of being a blessing to each other remain. Sometimes the seemingly smallest issues serve as examples of the universal situation, as illustrated in the question about the door between the nave and the narthex.

QUESTION   I am troubled that a door between the narthex and the nave of our church must remain closed to filter out noise before and during the service. I wish meditation time would allow people to flow into the service with the door open. Our church is so friendly that to be so noise-conscious seems out of character. What can be done to solve this problem?

RESPONSE Silence is important in worship, but silence is rarely the absence of sound. The silence of solitude enhances private devotions. When the people of God gather, there will be miscellaneous noise that can filter in and out of our meditative thoughts if we don't fight it. The worshipping community needs to consider the variety of needs of the people. Some can concentrate surrounded by all sorts of sound; others are aware of, and distracted by, everything around. Whether a door is open or shut may seem a small thing, but it represents the way a people of God deals with diversity.

The open door does, of course, invite people to move from fellowship to corporate worship. Still, your congregation's worship committee might discuss the architecture of the sanctuary and narthex, the variety of needs, and how best to meet them. Such discussion could lead to a richer use of other times of silence provided for in the liturgy: preceding the confession, after the sermon, and immediately before the benediction.

■ As seen in chapter 1, our difficulties in dealing with diversity are often focused in worship. They are expressed also in misunderstandings between generations, in the ways we organize and name our congregations, and in the ways we finance the work of the church. Just as the difficulty with an open or shut door reflects larger questions, so each question in this chapter often represents larger issues.

We will move through the life cycle by beginning with a question about bringing children to church. We move on to questions about youth, adulthood, and conclude with the visitation of shut-ins.

QUESTION In the baptismal liturgy on page 121 in *Lutheran Book of Worship*, the pastor says one should faithfully bring one's children to the services of God's house. It should add, ". . . and worship there with them." Some members bring their children to church, let them out, then go home believing they are living up to their promise. What is your opinion?

RESPONSE   The question addressed to sponsors and parents says "bring" not "take," "deposit," or "leave." It also says parents are to "teach them the Lord's Prayer, the Creed, and the Ten Commandments" so that their children "may lead godly lives." This is an awesome promise. Unfortunately some parents still see Baptism as having the child "done" rather than viewing it as the beginning of new life in Christ.

It is easy for parents to fall into the habit of simply dropping children at the church for Sunday school, especially when some congregations offer parents few opportunities for their own education. Members like yourself are needed to remind parents of their baptismal promises and to support their efforts to fulfill them. See that your congregation offers a wide variety of biblical and topical adult classes and invite the parents to go with you. Sit with young families in worship, sharing the responsibility of nurture by helping the children through the liturgy.

This said, it is useful to remember the words of a woman who frequently urged her pastors to welcome children, even if their parents did not attend church. This woman, an elder in her parish, said, "I was the child who was merely sent to Sunday school."

■   The congregation, united in Christ through Baptism, becomes a community of care that extends beyond family lines. We literally belong to each other. The readers' questions reflect this basic concept. Their concerns arise *because* they know they are responsible to and for each other. The following question is not so much filled with judgment as with frustration and even guilt.

QUESTION   What is happening to the young people in our Lutheran churches? Are there any youth programs or Bible studies after confirmation? It seems there are only bake sales, car washes, and other money-making projects so they can have more fun. Are we the only backsliders?

RESPONSE For you to consider young people's lack of spiritual growth as your congregation's "backsliding" is good. You care! Just as you face that challenge, so also many youth groups meet the challenge of attending national and regional Lutheran youth gatherings by earning money for the trip. These events, enormously exciting and fun, are frequently positive turning points in a young person's spiritual growth.

That is quite different, however, from young people or their adult advisors only raising money or only planning recreational events. Healthy youth ministry programs have a balance of ongoing education, community, service, worship, and recreation. Youth need opportunities to participate in all aspects of regular congregational life and to have separate youth activities to equip them to live out their faith in their daily lives where they face difficult decisions.

Youth groups who plan service projects will be growing in ministry skills while they serve. But in order to do that, congregations need to support them, not only with words, but with the congregation's budget. Youth ministers are needed who are fully recognized and supported by the church at large and by congregation members, like yourself, who care.

■ Congregations want to care about their members but find it is easier when there is little diversity in membership and lifestyle. Although the Gospels and the history of the early church make it clear that all people in all situations in life are to be included in the community of faith, such inclusion, particularly in public rites, is hard for some people to accept. Our rapidly changing society intensifies the difficulty.

QUESTION Is a large church wedding proper for a couple who each have been married and divorced? Both have children. I would approve of a small chapel wedding with an open house later for close relatives.

RESPONSE Christian congregations have an important opportunity at such weddings to move beyond propriety to the depths of Christian forgiveness and new life. The community gathers at weddings to witness, pray for, and pledge ongoing support for the couple. A second marriage should not be hidden, nor are children from a previous marriage an embarrassment. However, second marriages should not deny the reality of brokenness of previous marriages as though they did not exist. A Christian wedding is an occasion to remember the past with forgiveness and to make commitments for the future with trust.

■ A Christian community is a place for people to be who they really are. No reason to hide! The core of our life together is forgiveness in Jesus Christ. Living in that forgiveness and using its power for our acceptance of and interaction with each other is what congregational life is all about.

Since You Answered

One reader did not like our answer, however, and wrote: "Why doesn't our church practice what the Bible has to say? According to Romans 7:2-3 and 1 Corinthians 7:39, there should be no marriage until the first spouse dies." But in quoting Bible verses out of context, one misses their intent. In 1 Corinthians 7, Paul was giving his personal judgment on the wisdom of not marrying at all, writing that a woman is free to marry if her husband dies, "but in my judgment she is happier if she remains as she is" (v. 40 Revised Standard Version). In Romans, Paul was talking about living under grace, not law. The comments he gave about the death of a spouse are not in a discourse on marriage and divorce, but examples of the changing nature of the binding effect of a law. "Do you not know . . . that the law is binding on a person only during that person's life?" (Rom. 7:1). He went on to make his point, "Likewise . . . you have died to the law through the body of Christ, so that you may belong to another, to him who has been raised from the dead in order that we may bear fruit for God" (Rom. 7:4 RSV). We are not free to do whatever we want, but are discharged from the judging nature of the law, "dead to that which held us captive, so that we serve not under the old written code but in the new life of the Spirit" (v. 6 RSV). Living in the forgiveness of sins that we have in Christ's death and resurrection, we are to bear fruit, to live lives of responsible love and care.

■ As we move through the life cycle from Baptism and youth through marriage and family, we find some questions that deal with being adults together in a parish. One deals with the core decision-making body of the congregation, the church council. Specifically the issue was the proportion of women and men and the guidelines that help us at this turning point in history to use all the gifts of both genders for the work of the church.

QUESTION Does the Evangelical Lutheran Church in America have guidelines concerning the makeup of church councils, specifically the male-female balance? Our council consists of 12 adults and one teenager. Only three of the adults are women.

RESPONSE The ELCA model constitution for congregations says that "any voting member of the congregation may be elected" to the church council. It defines voting members as confirmed members. As a model, it does not give specific numbers for how many men and women should be on the council. Purpose statements include seeking "to involve all members of this congregation in worship, learning, witness, service, and support" and "to be examples individually and corporately of the style of life and ministry expected of all baptized persons." However, the ELCA constitution and bylaws do state that congregational representation at synod assemblies "shall be equally divided between male and female." Further, the Constitution for Synods states the synod council "shall establish processes that will ensure . . . that, as nearly as possible, 50 percent of the lay members of assemblies, councils, committees, boards or other organizational units shall be female and 50 percent shall be male," adding the minimum goal that 10 percent "be persons of color and/or persons whose primary language is other than English."

Equal representation of men and women on church councils also is an important goal. Your church council is three-fourths male. It is doubtful if this reflects the makeup of your congregation. Some congregations' councils have a disproportionately high number of women. Either situation reflects an imbalance. While calculating quotas may seem burdensome, some councils, boards, and committees now operating with more equal numbers feel a burden has been lifted and the group now feels "normal." A healthy distribution according to age and gender increases the possibility that a variety of perspectives and abilities will be brought to bear on council issues and actions.

■ As people move through life, retirement brings changes and choices. For many, longtime membership in a congregation is precious. They are reluctant to give up their role and responsibility. Yet, do they fully belong in their new community? Questions such as the following may increase.

QUESTION Longtime members of our congregation spend the winter in a warmer climate. They are active and enjoy sharing in the decision-making process, but they get very angry when decisions are made in their absence—especially ones with which they disagree. Who should make decisions: the travelers or our pastor and church council?

RESPONSE Christian congregations serve and live in specific places. The decisions they reach must fit the needs of their community and members in timely ways. As needs change, ways of operating must change.

To make the best choices, members need to be on the scene taking part in the work of the gospel. Congregational constitutions give the church council and pastor the responsibility for leading the ministry of the congregation. The work of the church cannot wait for absent members to participate. No decision should be postponed for this reason.

Let those who cannot vote write their opinions to the council for them to read and think about. But let the decisions be made when they need to be made.

Since You Answered

A few people responded, one with an opinion: "In the snowbird situation, the year 'round residents bring up important decisions or votes as soon as the snowbirds go south, thus effectively disenfranchising them." Such obvious and intentional exclusion is unloving and wrong.

Two writers had this suggestion: "Why are absentee ballots not acceptable in church as they are in civil voting?" and "The use of absentee ballots would make it possible for every member to take an active part in all the decisions of the congregation, even if he [or she] cannot attend the meetings."

The body of Christ is quite different from a civic voting precinct. In the church we pray for the Spirit to make us one. That does not mean fostering ways to keep us apart or leave people out of decision making. It dictates finding means to build the body, such as selecting times when people can be together and including opinions of those truly shut-in or unavoidably away. It means using methods of drawing forth ideas, listening, discussing, and coming to consensus that reflects all members of the body. It is often the discussion and the pursuit of consensus rather than an actual vote that is crucial in congregational meetings.

■ Older people are absent from the gathered people of God for other reasons. The following letter reflects the frustration of a homebound couple and the resulting dilemma about church membership.

QUESTION Because I don't drive, I rely on my husband to take me to our church. An ailment has kept him homebound for three weeks. I've not called my pastor because he is very busy and my husband is not critical. I've visited a church a block away. This week that pastor came to call. I'm uncomfortable. Was he recruiting?

RESPONSE Call your pastor and request he visit your ailing husband. Being homebound and cut off from worship is difficult for both of you. Tell your pastor and your parish of your need. Perhaps some members also will visit you or provide transportation to worship.

Your situation raises the issue of pastoral ethics and congregational cooperation. Your letter does not indicate if the nearby church is also Lutheran. If it is, you might consider membership there, not simply because of your present need, but because we belong to the church by virtue of Baptism. Membership in a local congregation is an expression of our being part of the whole church and should not be based on particular loyalties. The formation of the Evangelical Lutheran Church in America opens new possibilities for active membership in one's own neighborhood. Congregations need not compete with one another for members. Rather, they can cooperate in serving others, particularly those whose illnesses cut them off from the worshiping community.

It is good the local pastor responded to your presence in worship with a pastoral visit. Many pastors and congregations make follow-up calls on worship visitors as a standard part of their ministry.

■ One could multiply the numbers and types of questions, but all here carry a similar thread of the difficulty and desire to be the body of Christ. There may be no other gathering of people in our society that so encourages diversity and connects people at all ages and stages of life. Amid the questions the commitment is strong. We are called to belong to each other.

Another important issue in the congregation's life together is its identity. An ongoing dilemma for most congregations is how they financially support their mission and ministry. Within these concerns is the basic question: What face does the congregation present to the world? What is the witness we give by the way we live together? The first question in this group faces directly the issue of identity: the sign they place in front of the building.

QUESTION What are your views on a congregation's sign that simply shows a saint's name and the words "A Lutheran Parish Community"? The word *church* is omitted.

RESPONSE The phrase "a parish community" is being used occasionally, and there may be good reasons to encourage it. Lutherans do not often use the term *parish* because they do not tend to designate certain territory as a responsibility of a certain congregation. Lutherans have selected a congregation based on their likes and dislikes, not because they live in a certain area. This sometimes makes congregations compete for members.

Just as in the incarnation Jesus came to earth in a certain geographic place, so our ministry is specific, in a particular neighborhood or area. To say publicly that a group of Christians is a parish communicates responsibility for a certain locality for evangelism, shepherding, and mission.

Likewise, *community* reminds one that the church is not a building but the people of God who work together and gather regularly to worship and celebrate the sacraments. Such a congregation is, of course, a "church," a particular congregation of a Christian denomination. The New Testament concept of a church is the assembly of those called together by Christ, and it applies to the whole company of saints as well as to a house of Christian worship. The way a congregation identifies itself in its neighborhood speaks of how it understands its mission.

■ The final three questions of this chapter deal directly with giving. All relate to "fund-raising" and the deeper issues of talents, gifts, and stewardship.

QUESTION Are time, talent, and treasure of equal importance when giving to the church? Our pastor said our craft fair was not appropriate because it was an indirect way of giving. Many women would like to make craft items for the church to sell.

RESPONSE Time, talent, and treasure are equally significant, not only in what we give to the church, but also in the total offering of our daily lives to God. The check or money placed in the offering plate is a symbol of giving one's whole self to God.

Historically in the United States, husbands were considered the sole breadwinners, and married women often did not have their own money to give. Consequently, craft fairs and bazaars became a way women used their time and skills to contribute to the church's mission.

Fund-raising activities sometimes have appeared to absorb time and energy that could be spent in Bible study and service. Statements on stewardship and commercialism from the Evangelical Lutheran Church in America's predecessor church bodies suggest congregations should carefully examine all fund-raising projects by asking: Does the project inhibit commitment to Christian giving or shift responsibility for giving from the congregation to others? If the answer to either is yes, perhaps the fund-raising activity in question is not the best exercise of Christian responsibility.

Many congregations use money raised in commercial activities only for mission projects beyond the local congregation. Whether your congregation uses fund-raisers selectively or not at all, the church's mission of sharing the free gift of Jesus Christ must not be obscured.

QUESTION Our congregation is holding a raffle. Is this an appropriate fund-raising method for the church?

RESPONSE No. A statement of one of the Evangelical Lutheran Church in America's predecessor church bodies says, "Gambling has been described as involving three elements: (a) a valuable consideration, mutually risked in the hope of (b) winning a significant prize, which is awarded (c) not primarily for skill or ability but largely by the caprice of chance. . . . Congregations and charitable organizations should strive to keep their fund-raising practices free from appeals to unhealthy motivations such as greed or materialism. Appealing to people's greed in order to increase their charity is not a desirable style of fund-raising."

Congregations should not imitate gambling efforts because these events, especially when held under church leadership, legitimize gambling. Advertisements urging lottery participation and the news coverage of huge winnings leave no doubt that materialism drives gambling industries. In a state where lotteries and licensed track and off-track betting have been introduced recently, treatment for gambling addicts has become necessary.

The church is sustained primarily through members' free-will offerings. It needs to concentrate upon building a solid understanding of the priesthood of all believers. That priesthood, begun at our Baptism, involves a lifelong offering of ourselves to God through service to others. The promotion of gambling in the church absolutely contradicts the sacrificial nature of Christian living.

■ Whereas the previous two questions dealt with raising money, the following question looks at the issue of investing the congregation's money. This question, like many others involving the congregation, has hidden within it members' individual practices and communal decisions. People have different attitudes toward money and vary greatly in practice and responsibility. This complicates the task of deciding how to invest and manage our corporate congregational funds.

QUESTION As faithful Christians, should we contribute to endowment funds to safeguard our congregation's future? Are endowment funds good stewardship, or are ministry opportunities missed while large funds lie dormant? Should congregations invest when risk is involved?

RESPONSE We do not trust in endowment funds any more than we trust in insurance or our own labor to secure our congregation's future. All are ways we serve the God in whom we trust. Little is safe about mission or ministry. But there is a difference between risky investments and risk for the sake of the gospel. In a rapidly fluctuating stock market, this is clearer than ever.

Endowments are ways to be in mission in this generation and the next. They are most helpful, not when they attempt to bind the church, but when they allow and enable the people of God to determine the direction for mission. Such funds are not dormant. The money is at work. Further, these investments are not neutral. We need to give attention to our social responsibility in such investments. Church extension funds are a way to be deliberately engaged in mission elsewhere while caring for the future ministry in the local congregation.

People in heavily endowed congregations on occasion have thought their own small, regular offerings unnecessary. Endowments, however, can move people beyond a survival or maintenance mentality so that stewardship can be a way for them to freely and creatively offer themselves and their gifts to God.

■ These final questions about money conclude with an emphasis upon each person knowing he or she is absolutely indispensable to the work of ministry. All members, no matter how diverse or what their abilities, belong to each other and are needed by the congregation.

There will always be many questions to add to the category of congregational life. Hence, we have not added "Since You Didn't Ask" questions to this chapter. Chapter 4 deals with questions of biblical interpretation. At the core of our life together is our understanding of the Bible and the way the Bible guides our common life.

4

Interpretations of the Scriptures

Luther is supposed to have said, "Scripture is so shallow that a little child can wade in it, and so deep that a grown person can drown in it." We would add: "And it is a delight to swim around in it."

Lutherans are passionate about Scripture. We have inherited Luther's enthusiastic love for the Scripture's witness to Christ and the guidance Scripture provides for our life as the people of God. We agree that the Bible is the norm for our teaching and practice. But we differ when we ask *how* we interpret Scripture and in what way it guides us. Inquiries to "Since You Asked" often display this tension. Sometimes they are not so much questions as they are charges against the church.

Two questioners sent in nearly identical inquiries linking 2 Timothy 3:16 and 1 Timothy 2:14.

QUESTION Some Lutheran church bodies do not ordain women, using 1 Timothy 2:11-15 as their primary justification. Paul's reference to the way Adam and Eve were created and how Eve was deceived means this scripture reflects a deep theological truth, not merely a first-century bias. How can the Evangelical Lutheran Church in America ordain women in light of this and also 2 Timothy 3:16-17, which says all Scripture is inspired by God?

RESPONSE   The issue here is biblical interpretation and goes well beyond the ordination of women to the very being of women. Many interpreters isolate this text from its full context and therefore misunderstand its meaning.

In 1 Timothy 2:8, at the beginning of the paragraph in which this text stands, Paul makes clear that he is expressing his personal preference. He wrote, "I desire then that men (the Greek word is gender specific) should pray. . . ." Women are told to watch what they wear and do good deeds. They are not to preach, but they will be saved through childbearing if they continue in the faith.

In 1 Timothy 5:14 Paul uses the same expression: "I desire that younger widows marry, bear children, rule their households. . . ." But what of childless women, single or married? For nearly 2000 years women who have not given birth have been burdened with a sense of worthlessness. Does Paul really mean that only mothers can be saved?

Further, Paul's statement in 1 Timothy that Eve was deceived, not Adam, is hard to reconcile with Paul's statement in Romans 5:12-14 where he said sin "came into the world through one man"—Adam. Biblical interpretation involving this and other issues is not as simple as we might like.

Paul, in 1 Timothy, reflects a desire to continue the customs in which he had been trained before his conversion. He failed to see the full meaning of his own witness: "There is neither Jew nor Greek, slave nor free, male nor female; for you are all one in Christ Jesus" (Gal. 3:28). He was misled by the pharisaic tradition where men prayed, "God, I thank you that I was not born a woman."

He uses a traditional argument asserting that one should never discuss the Torah with women (a practice Jesus broke dramatically and often). Paul had opposed the pharisaic Christians who required circumcision. Having opposed the old law, would he be proposing a new law here? Paul clearly emphasizes that he is describing his pastoral preference and his own practice. We do injustice to Paul and to this text if we elevate his pastoral counsel to divine, unchangeable law.

But this inspired Scripture does teach us how pastors counsel their people. It also teaches us to receive pastoral counsel thoughtfully and critically, including this column's counsel. Pastors and the church are not infallible; they live by the grace of God. Paul, Martin Luther, pastors, and church councils can be wrong and need to be corrected by the heart of the faith—God's law and the gospel of God's unmerited grace.

Churches that use this text to prevent women's ordination need to be corrected. Misinterpreting this passage devalues women and hinders the church from fully using all the God-given gifts of women for ministry.

Since You Answered

Our response to this question evoked extensive comments from readers. Most were critical, although a few expressed appreciation for the answer's forthrightness. One of the positive notes added: "The Scriptures to which the author of 2 Timothy refers are the Hebrew Scriptures." The Scriptures Timothy knew from childhood were not the letters of St. Paul. (See 2 Timothy 3:15.)

But Lutherans include the generally accepted canon of the New Testament as also inspired and therefore take these texts seriously as the inspired Word of God—not excluding Paul's words in 1 Timothy 2:8. One printed response noted that the Evangelical Lutheran Church in America accepts the New Testament (including 1 Timothy) as the inspired Word of God and the *authoritative* source and norm. The writer continued, "If God couldn't keep Paul's personal preferences out of 1 Timothy, then how do we know if he was successful in Romans 6:23 or Ephesians 2:8, etc.?"

Not only did God not keep Paul's preferences out of 1 Timothy, God inspired him to say so.

There is no debate that these texts are inspired. This respondent and others keep overlooking those key words, "I desire," as equally inspired and equally profitable for our understanding of God's will. They mean what they say. What follows therefore describes Paul's pastoral preference. God inspired Paul to make that clear.

In 1 Corinthians 7, Paul drew even more explicit distinctions between his own desires and God's immutable will. In verse 8 Paul urged celibacy for the unmarried and for widows, conceding marriage only because of passion. If we believe that Paul's words are right for all times, we would now have to urge celibate life as the norm of the Christian's life and marriage as second best.

In the medieval church, Paul's argument for celibacy was included among the "counsels of perfection" and was applied to the clergy and to those who chose religious communities. Luther radically opposed this interpretation of Paul's position. He thought such a view minimized the Word when it sought to limit the counsels only to those thought to be more spiritually able. Luther saw Paul's advice for what it was; counsel from Paul for his day.

But these Pauline preferences are also inspired—as preferences—and we may learn from them. However, their authority is not as a new law. Rather, they describe a pastor's earnest advice to a troubled congregation. It was the best advice Paul could give considering his training, experience, and views on life.

Another respondent found it unbelievable that Paul could ever be wrong and need to be corrected. Quoting Acts 9:15 where God said, "he is a chosen instrument of mine to carry my name" and 2 Peter 3:15-16 where "Paul wrote to you according to the wisdom given him," the writer was dismayed. He wondered, "Who can claim a higher authority than God and thus claim to be superior to Paul?" He concluded, "I cannot accept that Paul is wrong. No wonder people are having problems with and are leaving the Evangelical Lutheran Church in America."

Paul's advice in 1 Timothy 2:11-15 and much of 1 Corinthians 7 is wrong for us. It was meant for the congregations of his day. Biblical study in the Evangelical Lutheran Church in America takes all of Scripture so seriously and trusts God so firmly that it can—and must—say that.

It is no claim of superiority over God or Paul, but a wholehearted faith that only God is infallible and that God used fallible people to write the Scriptures! Thank God that Paul made clear in 1 Timothy and 1 Corinthians that it was Paul, not God, who was advising.

As the church has continued to search the Scriptures to hear what God has to say, the church has repeatedly revised its understanding of what Scripture is saying to us. That's what the Reformation did! This has puzzled and upset many members who believe these interpretations could undermine their faith. God's authority continues in the midst of change. This truth provides assurance to the fearful and room for the faithful who continue to wonder and delight as they dig deeply into the Scriptures.

QUESTION We hear so much criticism of fundamentalists and literal Bible interpretation. Is it now considered naive or even heresy for Lutherans to believe that Adam and Eve were real people, that miracles really happened, that angels and demons really exist, that heaven and hell are real places, or that Moses wrote Genesis?

RESPONSE Some fundamentalists use the Bible to protect God, saying, "If you do not take every passage literally, you reject Christ." This limits how God speaks to us in Scripture.

It also limits God to say that sophisticated Christians cannot believe in miracles. God can and does perform miracles in ordinary as well as spectacular ways. Angels can and probably do exist. Evil is real, and we must deal with it. The demonic is not just some creature "out there."

In regard to your question about the first five books of the Bible, biblical scholars, except fundamentalists, tend to affirm that a more dynamic process involving multiple authors over many years was involved in the books' development.

For centuries the church believed in the actual existence of Adam and Eve. Recent scholarship suggests the significance of the Adam and Eve stories is not their literal truth or lack of it, but the theological points they make about the creation of humankind in God's image.

The difficulty lies in putting all such questions on the same plane. Questions about authorship or whether a particular story is best understood in a literal or a symbolic way are not on the same plane as questions about Jesus' identity and the salvation he accomplished.

The Bible is God's Word for faith and life. If someone believes Adam and Eve were historic people and this view is helpful to their Christian life, it is not good ministry to rip such a viewpoint from them. Nor should the faith of those who understand these stories in a symbolic way be questioned. The Christian community grows by searching the Scriptures together and upbuilding each other in faith.

Since You Answered

Most correspondents disagreed strongly with this position, but two expressed their appreciation. One noted, "I have always understood that regarding anything other than God as inerrant is idolatry."

Still, the majority of responses were represented in a letter that described our answer as "theological nonsense." It continued, "We either believe what God has given us throughout the ages or we do not. Creation did not just explode. . . . If this isn't what I am to believe, then I have been teaching the wrong Bible for the last 60 years."

Not the wrong Bible, but the wrong interpretation of God's inspired Word. We are not saved by our correct interpretation of the Bible; we are saved by grace. It is a hallmark of the Reformation that we continually search the Scriptures, always ready to be guided by the Spirit to acknowledge *our* errors, always seeking to find, not what we have always thought Scripture says, but what it actually does say.

Nor is the issue "either-or." It is fully possible to believe that God purposefully created the galaxies and still creates each of us while at the same time interpreting Genesis in a nonliteral manner.

Another writer insisted that the Mosaic authorship of the first five books of the Bible was unquestionable and that any thought of multiple authorship "drives people away from the means by which God speaks to people—the Word."

Several years ago an 80-year-old woman responded to a presenter of the Search Weekly Bible Studies on Genesis. He had asked her why she looked puzzled; Was she troubled? Her answer: "No. Well, yes." She had always wondered about the first books of the Bible, how they had been written, and if Moses could really have been the only author. When the presenter explained a little more about biblical sources, the woman responded, "What really bothers me is why they haven't told us this before." This woman had long been a careful student and faithful believer of God's Word. Taking God's Word seriously meant she had long puzzled over it and without external influence had noticed the multiple strands in Genesis.

■ Lutherans care passionately about the Bible and its place in our teaching, worship, and life. But often we fail to ask some fundamental questions about the Scriptures. We assume the Bible is composed of the 39 books of the Hebrew Scriptures and the 27 books we know as the New Testament. Yet Lutherans have never formally established this list, which is called a *canon*. One inquirer was intrigued by a set of writings most Lutherans have not encountered.

QUESTION The books of the Apocrypha are mentioned in the back of my Bible. The reference noted that "in Luther's German translation . . . (1534), the Apocrypha [stand] between the Old and New Testaments." Has the Lutheran church examined these books? Where can I find them?

RESPONSE The books of the Apocrypha were not included in the Hebrew Scriptures, were never formally recognized (although highly regarded) by the Eastern church, and were not accepted as part of the Bible in the Western church as late as 420 A.D. It was not until the post-Reformation Council of Trent, completed in 1563, that the Roman Catholic Church, with certain exceptions, declared them canonical.

Canon is the Greek word for *measure*. Hence the canonical books are those that measure or rule teachings of the Christian church. The Apocrypha has been carefully examined by Lutheran scholars ever since the Reformation. Lutherans have followed Luther's dictum that the Apocrypha is "not the equal to the Holy Scriptures, . . . yet . . . profitable and good to read."

You may find the Apocrypha in Roman Catholic translations and in an ecumenical study Bible, *The New Oxford Annotated Bible with the Apocrypha*. Page xix of this edition's "Introduction to the Apocrypha" notes that the hymn "Now Thank We All Our God" is dependent on Luther's translation of the apocryphal book Sirach (50:22-24).

■ Luther's attitude toward those books we generally consider canonical may astonish some Lutherans. Since Luther valued the books according to the extent Christ was proclaimed, he classified the books of James, Jude, Hebrews, and Revelation as a kind of unnecessary appendix. Luther's radical rule reveals a basic approach toward Scripture: We believe the Scriptures because they bear witness to Jesus Christ.

In addition to the Old Testament Apocrypha, there are numerous other works written before and after the New Testament that are generally agreed to be pious imitations or attempts to mislead people. They, too, are informative, and much may be learned from them but they, along with the Apocrypha, do not rule the teachings of the church.

Concern about the Bible permeates all our life together as Lutherans. Therefore it is not surprising that readers want to understand puzzling translations in their worship life. Change in such central elements of our life as the Bible and worship can be unsettling.

QUESTION Why do the Psalms differ in the hymnals of the Evangelical Lutheran Church in America and the Lutheran Church–Missouri Synod? I suppose two different biblical translations are used. But why do some Psalms have different numbers of verses? Perhaps more doctrinally important, why do the Psalms in the *Lutheran Book of Worship* not end with the trinitarian Gloria Patri, "Glory to the Father and to the Son and to the Holy Spirit"?

RESPONSE On the advice of Lutheran Old Testament scholars, those who prepared the *Lutheran Book of Worship* chose the translation of the Psalms used in the *Episcopalian Book of Common Prayer* for reasons of faithfulness to the Hebrew text, poetic beauty, and ecumenism. The Missouri Synod's hymnal, *Lutheran Worship*, uses the translation from the *New International Version* of the Bible. Regarding numbering, the original Hebrew text was not numbered. Numbering of verses is a relatively late addition to help the user and varies among translations. The *LBW* includes 122 of the 150 psalms. *Lutheran Worship* includes 60. In addition, *LW* includes selected psalm verses with tone assigned and printed by the text as the Introit in the Propers for the Day.

The Gloria Patri was used to make the Christian use of a psalm explicit. In services when communion is not celebrated, psalm prayers written for each of the 122 psalms included in *LBW* serve this purpose. These are found in the *LBW Minister's Desk Edition*. In the eucharistic service, the psalm serves as a bridge from the Old Testament lesson to the second lesson. This immediate context makes its use clearly Christian.

■ We are asked about surprisingly few specific biblical passages, other than those that have been used as doctrinal prooftexts, but we do receive a few specific questions.

QUESTION Some of us in our study group are puzzled about what Luke's Gospel means when Jesus says, "Everyone who speaks a word against the Son of Man will be forgiven; but [whoever] blasphemes against the Holy Spirit will not be forgiven" (Luke 12:10).

RESPONSE   You are not alone in your puzzling. Theologians of the early church wrestled with this text and similar sayings in Matthew 12:32 and Mark 3:28-29. Sometimes people have feared they were guilty of an unknown misdeed and have despaired of their salvation.

To understand Jesus' words, it is important to look at what God's Spirit does. In the Apostle's Creed, we see some of the Spirit's work: "I believe in the Holy Spirit, the holy catholic church, the communion of saints, the forgiveness of sins. . . ." The Spirit draws us into community through the people of God to share God's mercy with us. The Holy Spirit gives us repentance, even if we speak against Jesus. But we can resist the Spirit. God does not force love upon us. To blaspheme the Spirit is to say we do not need God's mercy. Luke makes this clear in Stephen's speech (Acts 7:51). It is like our speaking against a friend. Others remind us of our friend's love for us in order to change our heart. They encourage us to renew our friendship. In many and various ways the Spirit befriends us, reminding us of God's unfathomable love in Jesus Christ and encouraging us to live and grow in it.

If someone in your group is disturbed about this, you might suggest they talk with their pastor.

■   It is good to hear readers are wrestling together with the meaning of Scripture. Years ago a Canadian pastor described the approach of one of his retired members to problems in understanding difficult biblical passages. Upon hearing that his member was regularly reading the Bible, he asked, "What do you do when you come across some troubling passages?" His member replied: "When we farmed in Stony Plain, our family went out every spring to dig up stones so the plow would not hit them. Some stones the children could dig out and lift, some my wife could remove, and some I was able to extract. Some we could unearth as we worked together. But there were many difficult stones, too deeply imbedded for any of us. Those we would leave for next spring when God's frost might push them further out of the earth. I study God's Word in the same way.'' The faith of this farmer is an excellent model for all who seriously delight in the holy Scriptures.

Since You Didn't Ask

So many questions focus on controversial issues. It may be that some members are so certain what Scriptures say that they have difficulty learning anything new. Others seem to fear the Scriptures are too hard to understand. The next question might have been asked.

QUESTION Some members of our congregation seem bored with Scripture study. They find nothing new in the stories they learned as children. Other members are afraid they will not be able to understand what they read. Can you help us?

RESPONSE The Swedish church faced this issue several decades ago. It offered an approach known as the Vasteras method. Where it has been used, it helps laity overcome their fear that they cannot use the Bible. This approach aims to encourage readers to delight in, to search, to approach Scripture as God's love letter.

The method is simple. As a portion of Scripture is read, either aloud or silently, either in a group or in privacy, every person makes marks in the margin of the text.

The marks may vary, and readers can make up their own. An exclamation point notes an exciting passage. A light bulb (or a candle) marks a new thought triggered by the Scripture. Down arrows note a text that depresses, up arrows a passage that gives the reader joy. Question marks highlight puzzling sentences.

After the section has been read, the group shares, verse by verse, the marks they have made. In large groups, the first discussion sometimes is held in smaller subgroups to encourage sharing.

While it sounds highly personal (it is), this method does not remain individualistic. Members of the class share their reactions with each other. They learn that others gain insights that they do not have—and so gain appreciation for the richness of Scriptures. They encounter differing reactions to the passages—and are encouraged to rethink their conclusions. They meet puzzling verses—and are stimulated to search further through Scripture and draw upon the gifts scholarly study offers.

■ Another problem some people have voiced—but have not written in to ask—is that Scripture seems fragmented to them. They see few connections. Perhaps this is a question they might have asked.

QUESTION   Many of our people remember the stories from Sunday school about Samson, Adam and Eve, Solomon, Ruth, Jesus' birth, the boy Jesus in the temple, the good Samaritan, and so forth. But they have trouble seeing them as much more than morality tales, telling people how to be good. For example, they see the point of the story of the boy Jesus in the temple as "remember to tell your parents where you are." So they feel little need to study these texts again. They consider them boring. How should we study them?

RESPONSE   Using this example, it might be good to begin with the picture frame (the surrounding verses) into which that story is set. Skip the story—to begin with—and look at Luke 2:39-40 and 51-52. Let the people puzzle over the contrast between verse 40 and 52. What does it mean that Jesus was filled with wisdom (v. 40) and Jesus grew in wisdom (v. 52)? This may help them begin to see that Luke wanted to say more about who Jesus was than to provide a behavior model.

The resistance may be deeper, however. It may be that some prefer a simple interpretation of the text because they fear their faith will be undermined if they meet a different way of seeing the stories. Some fear that if they have been wrong they may have been unbelieving. Others rightly fear that they will be facing a challenge to a childish faith—and that faith may need challenging. A faith securely grounded in Christ can be open to growth, to change, to deeper insight as one grows.

Luther's basic insight that Scriptures are the cradle of Christ and that all are meant to press home Jesus may help them. In Scripture study as a whole, it is good to make clear that Christ—a gracious Christ—is the center. Lutherans study Scripture as they do theology: to see the meaning of Jesus in the world and in the life of the people of God.

5

Issues concerning Theological Beliefs

Article 2.05 of the constitution of the Evangelical Lutheran Church in America states the confession that binds the people of this church together: "This church accepts the Unaltered Augsburg Confession as a true witness to the gospel, acknowledging as one with it in faith and doctrine all churches that likewise accept the teachings of the Unaltered Augsburg Confession." This statement is not exclusive, but it sets boundaries for a common faith. Christians want to know what their church believes. Although there are many differences among the church's members, the Augsburg Confession sets forth articles of faith "as a true witness to the gospel." These Lutheran confessions are acknowledged in ordination rites and written into constitutions of congregations.

In this chapter, church members' questions are arranged to correspond to the articles of the Augsburg Confession as found in *The Book of Concord*. Excerpts from the Augsburg Confession are quoted. Obviously the Augsburg Confession does not speak directly to particular contemporary situations, but the topics parallel the basic articles. We commend the Augsburg Confession and the entire *Book of Concord* to congregations for regular study.

Article I (God)[1]: . . . There is one divine essence, which is called and which is God, eternal, incorporeal, indivisible, of infinite power, wisdom, and goodness, the maker and preserver of all things, visible and invisible. . . ."

QUESTION With utter disgust I read of the contest in *The Lutheran* for young people to define God. Whatever happened to the definition of God we memorized from the explanation of Martin Luther's *Small Catechism* (Augsburg Publishing House, 1946)? It said: "God is an incomprehensible and immutable Spirit, who is eternal, almighty, omniscient, omnipresent; He is also wise, good, merciful, holy, true and righteous." Aren't these definitions good enough? Children need Bible verses to verify their answers so they will know if they are right or wrong.

RESPONSE God is beyond human definition. We need to expand our concepts of God throughout our lifetime. As we grow in faith and search the Scriptures, our questions deepen, sometimes changing perceptions which were appropriate for one age but are inappropriate for another.

The "Youngchurch" page (*The Lutheran*, July 13, 1988) invited young readers not to "define" but to share their "view of God." The large number of responses (2,144) gave evidence that many young people think about the meaning of God for their lives (see the Oct. 21, 1988, issue, pp. 16-21).

What the Church teaches children about God through parents and teachers is important. It is also important to know what children are already thinking about.

Continuing to explore Scripture, considering the reality of God in this world, and beholding in awe God's love for us are

---

1. Quotations from the Augsburg Confession are from *The Book of Concord: The Confessions of the Evangelical Lutheran Church,* trans. and ed. Theodore G. Tappert (Philadelphia: Fortress Press, 1959). The Augsburg Confession is a confession of faith presented in Augsburg by certain princes and cities to His Imperial Majesty Charles V in the year 1530. The titles of articles were inserted in and after 1533.

good for people of all ages. Not surprisingly, the images submitted by these young Lutherans pictured God as creator, savior, and protector. Their "views" showed the mercy, holiness, omniscience, and omnipresence of God which you also learned and hold dear.

Memorizing Scripture and Luther's *Small Catechism* is a good thing. It helps us root our understanding of God deep in the faith. But learning Bible passages out of context or just to prove ourselves right or wrong is not helpful. The biblical witness is intended to allow us to know God and how God relates to humankind. It enables us to consider God's reality and behold God's love for us.

■ Adults as well as children have a wide range of images of God in their minds. We do not need to be afraid to discuss our changing concepts of God. In fact, an adult forum might be a good place to simply ask one another, "Who is God for you? What images or actions of God are part of your daily life?" When Sunday morning forums are composed of people from nearly every decade of adulthood, listening intently to one another can be very helpful. The Christian community, well-steeped in God's self-revelation in the Bible, well-rehearsed in hymns of praise, can provide any needed corrective. God *is* beyond human definition; sharing a common confession of faith, we find it good to grow in our concepts of God.

Article 3 (The Son of God): ". . . Christ . . . was born of the virgin Mary, truly suffered, was crucified, dead, and buried, that he might reconcile the Father to us. . . ."

QUESTION I heard a protestant preacher say Jesus was born so he could die on the cross. That was a new one to me. Is he right?

RESPONSE Jesus was born to live for us. If Jesus was born simply to die, then Herod's soldiers could have killed him as a baby. The cross is central to our preaching because it shows the depth of God's love for us. Jesus' rising assures us that death, God's last enemy, does not have the last word.

Some preaching focuses on Jesus' death as payment to God's wrath. This approach stresses guilt as a barrier to our entry into heaven. There is truth here, but this is only one of many ways the Scriptures proclaim the meaning of Jesus for us. For instance, the Gospel according to John emphasizes Jesus as God's gift of love to the world, that the world might have life.

Scripture also says the fear of death and the burden of guilt bar the way to the new life that begins here and now. Jesus was born among us, walked in our midst, laughed, cried, prayed, overturned tables, and ate with sinners and tax collectors. Christ lived aware of death, but was not ruled by the fear of death. Jesus' death on the cross (a death he did not seek), liberates us from the fear of death. In the resurrection, the Christ returned to his fearful disciples and set them free to risk their lives serving others.

Since You Answered

A number of readers responded to this question, quoting Bible passages to assert their faith. One reader quoted Jesus: "Now is my soul troubled. And what shall I say? 'Father, save me from this hour'? No, for this purpose I have come to this hour" (John 12:27). The reader went on to cite a number of hymns ending with, "The Son of man also came not to be served but to serve, and to give his life as a ransom for many" (Mark 10:45).

Another person wrote, "If Jesus' dying was just to 'show the depth of God's love' . . . Jesus could have died a natural death." Jesus' unjust death—he was misunderstood by his disciples, rejected by his people, falsely accused by the authorities, abandoned by the government, and even "forsaken" by God—was essential to free us from our fear of a wrathful God. But God's wrath is the underside of God's love, love that cried out on the cross, "Forgive them, they know not what they do."

76

Another reader said, "Christ's death was planned since the Fall in the Garden of Eden and before the foundation of the world because of sin." Yes, Christ's death was needed, a tragic necessity, and yes, God knew it. But to see Christ's death as a cut-and-dried fact is to lose sight of the pain-filled, human dimension of his death and resurrection.

Christ's death was inevitable because of the pervasiveness and power of sin, but Jesus was not simply going through the motions, carrying out a prewritten script as though it were only a play. It was not just a death *scene*. The agony of Christ was real. We can become so accustomed to saying, "Jesus died on the cross for my sin," that we miss the depth of that confession. His death was in the face of life. Life was the goal and the gain. Jesus, like all human beings, was born to live—and yet he died for us. Realizing this, we see his death as more tragic, more profound, and his resurrection more powerful.

■ Just as the previous question goes to the core of the faith, so does the following question, which deals with salvation.

Article IV (Justification): "It is also taught among us that we cannot obtain forgiveness of sin and righteousness before God by our own merits, works, or satisfactions, but that we receive forgiveness of sin and become righteous before God by grace, for Christ's sake, through faith. . . ."

Article VI (The New Obedience): "Our churches also teach that this faith is bound to bring forth good fruits and that it is necessary to do the good works commanded by God."

QUESTION What does "being saved" mean for Lutherans? I know of others who believe they cannot be saved unless they give up smoking, drinking, and are sanctified.

RESPONSE Lutherans understand salvation as new life in Christ that begins now and is completed in heaven. New life begins with

God's unconditional acceptance of us. It is not dependent on our actions, including giving up smoking and drinking. God's love in Christ calls us to grow in love and service of others. This includes caring for our own bodies. Smoking is harmful and we do well to avoid it. But this is not a requirement for "being saved" and does not disqualify us as Christians. If perfect lives are required for salvation, no one can be saved. The "Brief Order for Confession and Forgiveness" reminds us of our continuing need for forgiveness with the words: "If we say we have no sin, we deceive ourselves . . ." (1 John 1:8).

The term *sanctified* as used by holiness churches usually means an instantaneous act of sanctification where God quickly makes one totally perfect. Lutheran teaching, however, reminds us that we always need to grow in love and service. This is why we pray, "For the sake of your Son, Jesus Christ, have mercy on us. Forgive us, renew us, and lead us, so that we may delight in your will and walk in your ways. . . ."

Since You Answered

A member of a holiness church responded to the column: "There are many churches that believe, as mine does, that sanctification is both instantaneous and gradual . . . and that sanctification does not deliver us from the infirmities, ignorance, and mistakes that are common to people." It is helpful to hear directly from Christians concerning their church's beliefs and practices, although the reader does not include "sin" among the list of "weaknesses" that the sanctified have in common with the rest of humanity.

Another reader, a Christian for only 11 months, was concerned that we had not said enough about salvation, adding that the entire year she had attended a Lutheran church, no one ever came up to ask if she was saved or knew what the gospel was. The point is well taken that Lutherans often take for granted that central part of their faith that is so dear, neglecting to speak about it often in daily conversation.

The reader wrote that she found it hard to believe that God unconditionally accepts us. It is because of God's unconditional love that God came in Jesus Christ to live and die and be raised for us! Jesus is a gift. The Spirit's work of faith is a gift. It is not our asking Are you saved? or answering this question correctly that assures us of salvation. But, indeed, as the confessions say, such faith is "bound to bring forth good works" and witness to such a great gift.

■ The Holy Spirit also puts us into communion with all others who believe in Jesus Christ:

Article VII (The Church): "It is also taught among us that one holy Christian church will be and remain forever. . . . It is as Paul writes in Eph. 4:4-5, 'There is one body and one Spirit, just as you were called to the one hope that belongs to your call, one Lord, one faith, one baptism' " (RSV).

QUESTION When I learned the catechism in German, we said, "I believe in the holy Christian church." Now the *Lutheran Book of Worship* says, "I believe in . . . the holy catholic church." Why was this changed?

RESPONSE It is unfortunate when the word *catholic* becomes equated with the Roman Catholic tradition because we lose the word's richness. In the 15th century, the original term *catholic* was translated *Christian*. The *Lutheran Book of Worship* is a restoration of the original.

The terms *holy* and *catholic* describe the nature of the Christian church. That is, each word helps us see what the church is like.

The Christian church is holy because God proclaims it holy. It is also catholic, or all-encompassing and universal. This word declares the Christian church is not limited to any corner of the world. It also emphasizes that the Christian church includes all sorts of people: rich and poor, women and men, and people of every race and of all nations. Reclaiming the word *catholic* in our creeds stretches our awareness of the fullness of the Christian church.

■ There were many responses; we therefore included a follow-up question in a later column:

QUESTION Why can't you pastors and theologians, who are supposed to know more than we lay people, get the point we are trying to get across? We know *catholic* means "universal," but the word *universal* does not guarantee everything in our church is Christian. Cults also use this word. Also, *Christian* is clearer.

RESPONSE We hear your frustration. Leaders sometimes do not listen far enough into someone's question to really hear what is being asked. Likewise, persistent questioning may be a refusal to accept an answer, or it may be a sincere desire to continue to learn and grow. No one of us has all knowledge, which is one reason why we need to listen to each other and remember we are part of the larger universal—catholic—church.

Names do not guarantee everything is Christian. Even the word *Christian,* although clearer, may be used by a cult that does not believe the grace of God in Jesus Christ is central. The word *catholic*, which, as you know, means "universal," reminds us we are part of a global Christian family and keeps us from perceiving ourselves in an ingrown, small way.

Since You Answered

Readers seemed unappeased. A number suggested that if *catholic* does mean "universal" (to many people *catholic* has come to mean "Roman Catholic") why don't we simply say *universal?* However, *catholic* means "universal" and more. It means not only "world-wide," but also "across time and totally inclusive of all peoples and all races." One person said, "We have one dear man in our congregation who says, 'It really doesn't matter what they print for us to say. I always say the creed in Norwegian anyway!' "

Interest in the term *catholic* and the great desire to distinguish Lutherans from Roman Catholics is understandable when one recalls that many Lutherans frequently heard anti-Roman Catholic statements in preaching and teaching when they were young. It is difficult to believe in one Lord, one faith, and one Baptism when divisions remain, but we are called to believe the church is a gift and is one in the midst of difficulty.

■ The Augsburg Confession goes on about the nature of the Church.

Article VIII (What is the Church?): "Properly speaking, the church is the assembly of saints and true believers. . . ."

QUESTION In the Evangelical Lutheran Church in America we hear a lot about inclusivity. Is the priesthood of all believers or universalism the basis of an inclusive church?

RESPONSE Inclusivity has nothing to do with universalism but much to do with the priesthood of all believers. It is central to the gospel of Christ and has its base in all three articles of the Apostles' and Nicene Creeds.

The Creator God has lovingly made a wide variety of human beings differing in color, sex, age, and ability. Each is unique, yet designed to work together. Because of our sin, we fear and sometimes hate the differences God has created.

In Christ our alienation is removed and we become gifts to one another. The Holy Spirit calls all believers to the tasks of ministry, not according to race or gender, but according to the gifts God has given. An inclusive church seeks these gifts and insights so that the church may minister faithfully in the world.

■ From God, salvation, and the church, the Augsburg Confession moves on to talk about Baptism. Christians have questions about Baptism today, too, although the issues may differ.

Article IX (Baptism): "Our churches teach that Baptism is necessary for salvation, that the grace of God is offered through Baptism, and that children should be baptized. . . ."

QUESTION Our congregation's policy statement on Baptism reads: "Private baptisms do not reflect our Lutheran understandings of the sacrament and will occur only under pressing medical circumstances." It also emphasizes that the assembled congregation commits itself to the new member. While I agree 100 percent, I cannot quite say why. What do you think?

RESPONSE Baptism involves a public confession of faith. In the church's infancy, Baptism was ministered primarily to adults who made public confession after a period of instruction. The stories of Nicodemus and of some believing authorities in John 3 and in John 12:42 reflect the desire of some to keep their faith in Jesus private. In John 3:21 and in numerous other sayings, Jesus insisted that faith be public, not hidden (like a candle under a basket)! Private baptisms contradict the public nature of faith and Christ's body in the world.

The custom of private Baptism arose as faith became more private and individual. Baptism even came to be seen by some as an intrusion into congregational worship. Unfortunately, some pastors even discourage baptisms within the liturgy.

When an adult or child is baptized into Christ, they are joined with the body of Christ. This work of the Holy Spirit ordinarily is carried out through the pastor, who represents the whole church, and with the full participation of the worshipers present.

Also, we cannot sustain a growing, serving faith without the support, encouragement, correction, and prayers of our sisters and brothers in Christ. We cannot walk the way of Christ alone.

We need each other. In Baptism Christ binds our lives together and gives us sisters and brothers. Each baptism in which we participate reminds us of God's gift of salvation; it gives us to each person baptized as a partner in the pilgrimage of faith.

■ Theology is never done in a vacuum. Questions are raised in the context of the problems of the day. In Luther's time the boundaries of church and society were virtually the same. There existed a "Christendom." In the 20th-century United States of America, there is a significant gulf between people's Sunday faith communities and other weekday communities of which they are a part (more will be said about this in chapter 8). The modern overemphasis on individualism is cause for concern among Christians, as well as is the tendency to keep the church in the private sphere and Christian life disconnected from public life. In such a context, public Baptism with the support of the Christian community is vital.

The Augsburg Confession moves on to discuss the Lord's Supper, confession, repentance, use of the sacraments, and ecclesiastical order and rites. The subject of ministry, Articles V and XIV, is more fully discussed in chapter 2 in this book. Church rites are discussed in chapter 1. Article XVI on civil government is touched on in chapter 8. The next question relates to Article XVII.

Article XVII (The Return of Christ to Judgment): "It is also taught among us that our Lord Jesus Christ will return on the last day for judgment and will raise up all the dead, to give eternal life and everlasting joy to believers and the elect but to condemn ungodly [people] and the devil to hell and eternal punishment. . . ."

QUESTION Why doesn't the Lutheran church talk or preach more about the second coming of Jesus Christ? Is there any way to be ready for Jesus' second coming?

RESPONSE Lutherans do not stress the images of Jesus' return with clouds, so perhaps it appears we do not talk about his second coming. But we confess each Sunday that he will return to judge the living and the dead. We believe the best way to be prepared is to trust and serve Christ in our daily lives. Luther, when asked what he would do if he knew Jesus was coming the next day, is reported to have said, "I would plant another apple tree." He meant that our preparation is not focused on the future but on living this life in Christ.

In the familiar judgment parable in Matthew 25, the faithful are surprised when the returning Savior says, "I was hungry and you gave me food, I was thirsty and you gave me drink, I was a stranger and you welcomed me, I was naked and you clothed me, I was sick and you visited me, I was in prison and you came to me" (RSV). They were simply doing what they knew needed to be done. The best way to prepare for the second coming is to trust Christ and serve people in need. Lutherans teach and preach this unfailingly.

■ A reader responded that we need to hear more about the second coming, and perhaps we do. Lutherans, perhaps in contrast to some other religious bodies, speak infrequently about the second coming. The emphases of such groups are frequently on the "when" rather than on the service we are to be about now. Another danger is linking the second coming with a militaristic view that accepts nuclear war as inevitable and even part of God's plan to hasten the second coming. Christ nowhere advocates hurting people in order to hasten the coming of the kingdom. Christ will come. Our calling is to love the world's people and fill our waiting with ministry.

The Augsburg Confession speaks further about the works we are to do while we wait. Confidence that Christ will return enables us to minister freely.

Article XX (Faith and Good Works): "Our teachers have been falsely accused of forbidding good works. . . . Since the teaching about faith, which is the chief article in the Christian life, has been neglected so long (as all must admit) while nothing but works was preached everywhere. . . . It is also taught among us that good works should and must be done. . . . Without faith and without Christ human nature and human strength are much too weak to do good works, call upon God, have patience in suffering, love one's neighbor, diligently engage in callings. . . ."

QUESTION Why is the Athanasian Creed in the *Lutheran Book of Worship* (pp. 54-55)? We know our salvation comes by grace, "not because of works, lest [anyone] should boast" (Eph. 2:9). Yet this creed states: "all people shall rise bodily to give an account of their own deeds. Those who have done good will enter eternal life, those who have done evil will enter eternal fire. . . . One cannot be saved without believing this firmly and faithfully." Please explain this contradiction.

RESPONSE The Athanasian Creed is one of the three ancient Christian creeds of the Church to which Lutherans subscribe. The others are the more familiar Apostles' and Nicene Creeds. The Athanasian Creed is sometimes used on Trinity Sunday because its primary purpose is to defend the doctrine of the Trinity and the incarnation of God in Christ.

You cite a portion of the creed that says nothing different than what Jesus said in the parable of the judgment in Matthew 25: "Come . . . inherit the kingdom prepared for you from the foundation of the world; for I was hungry and you gave me food, I was thirsty and you gave me drink, I was a stranger and you welcomed me, I was naked and you clothed me, I was sick and you visited me, I was in prison and you came to me" (RSV). Similarly Jesus said, "Depart from me, you cursed, into the eternal fire prepared for the devil and the devil's angels. . . . As you did it not to the least of these, you did it not to me" (RSV).

Both faith and works are God's gracious gifts. Therefore, we cannot boast of our good works. They can be done only as we trust that God loves and forgives us. If we do not trust God's care for us, we can care for no one but ourselves, and even that is distorted. But when we trust God, we can love ourselves and risk loving each other. Faith and works go together, even as the passage from Ephesians 2 that you cited continues: "For we are [God's handiwork], created in Christ Jesus for good works, which God prepared beforehand, that we should walk in them" (v. 10).

■ In a confessional church there is strength in common belief, but there is also the danger that as differences arise, churches divide. Lutherans have a sad history of people hurting each other over actual and perceived differences of doctrine. The following seeks to clarify rumors of false doctrine and practice.

QUESTION There are rumors in my congregation that the Evangelical Lutheran Church in America believes in universalism, does not believe in the virgin birth, the resurrection, or in the inerrancy of the Bible, and that it will allow practicing homosexuals to serve as pastors. Are these rumors true?

RESPONSE Gently correct those who believe the rumors you have heard, because the rumors are false. The eighth commandment is being broken; false witness is being spread.

The ELCA not only affirms the Apostles', Nicene, and Athanasian creeds in its constitution, but also confesses them in its recognized orders of worship. These creeds acknowledge Jesus Christ as the virgin-born, risen Savior of all people. The ELCA teaches and the creeds affirm that salvation is through Jesus Christ and none other, rejecting universalism totally.

The ELCA's confession of faith also declares: "This church accepts the canonical Scriptures of the Old and New Testaments as the inspired Word of God and the authoritative source and norm of its proclamation, faith, and life." The framers of the confession, following the insights of many Lutheran theologians, believe this is a more accurate understanding of God's intention for the Scriptures than the term *inerrancy*. The non-Lutheran, 19th-century concept of inerrancy leads to many unhelpful misunderstandings and questions like: Inerrant in what way? Is the Bible inerrant in matters of history, genealogy, and astronomy?

These questions lead directly away from the Scriptures's purpose, which is to declare Christ to us that we may believe and be saved. The Bible is the Word of God and the source and norm of the church's life not because it gives us unerring information, but because God continues to speak through it. The ELCA is dedicated to enabling its members to study the Bible in order to grow in faith and service.

In regard to your final concern, statements by ELCA Bishop Herbert W. Chilstrom and actions by the ELCA Conference of Bishops have made it clear that the ELCA will not allow practicing homosexuals to serve as pastors nor will it "knowingly ordain a practicing homosexual."

Encourage those disturbed by these rumors to speak with their pastor and bishop.

Since You Answered

Although that question and response involved very controversial and emotional topics, reader reaction was over one phrase in particular: "The non-Lutheran, 19th-century concept of inerrancy." Two readers pointed out accurately that there is an earlier history of that concept that goes back to the Jews and early Christians. St. Augustine made it normative for catholic Christianity, and Lutheran theologians of the late 16th and 17th centuries used the term, but it was not a confessional position of Lutherans. In the last century, however, new questions raised by biblical scholarship brought a reaction in American Lutheranism which sought to use the idea of verbal inspiration as the first line of defense.

■   And so it is that controversies over doctrines and terms continue. The Augsburg Confession concludes: "These are the chief articles that are regarded as controversial. Although more abuses could be mentioned, to avoid undue length we have discussed only the principal ones." Issues of great significance in one age may in another time seem trivial. The people of God in every age strive to be faithful people; hence God's people continue to discuss theology. The constitution of the ELCA says, "The church confesses the Gospel, recorded in the Holy Scriptures and confessed in the ecumenical creeds and Lutheran confessional writings, as the power of God to create and sustain the Church for God's mission in the world" (2:07). Theology is never for its own sake, but for the sake of mission and ministry.

6

Questions about
the Faith of Others

In the Nicene Creed we confess, "one Lord, one faith, one Baptism." Baptism is the watermark of the Church. There is one Christian Baptism, administered by those who confess faith in one Lord, the holy Trinity. The pouring of baptismal water with the Word marks the baptized as members of one family and separates them from those who are not joined with Christ into the body of Christ.

In this rapidly changing society, the church is changing, too. The formation of the Evangelical Lutheran Church in America heightened the fear of change for many members. Members of all the predecessor church bodies encountered new names, new leaders, and new ways of doing things. The new Lutheran church body was intended to be more than a merger, it was intended to be something new. It is not surprising that numerous questions have come into the column about the Evangelical Lutheran Church in America, and in particular about its relationships with other Christians and other religious communities.

QUESTION The leadership of our church appears to have made priorities of ecumenism and the recruitment of minorities (at whatever cost to traditional worship). It also appears they want to insert themselves into this country's politics. This points toward the death of Lutheranism. Why don't they acknowledge that Lutheranism takes last place against these other objectives, be honest about what they are doing, and remove *Lutheran* from the name of this church?

RESPONSE   Your question displays a passionate concern, but it also reveals a sad misunderstanding of Lutheranism. These "other objectives" are Lutheran to the core. Working together with our sister and brother Christians at home and abroad, reaching out to all people with the gospel, and speaking to social issues are as Lutheran as Luther.

Luther sought to work closely with Greek Orthodox churches. He also tried to evangelize the Turks and the Jews. On the controversial political issue of monopolies, Luther wrote: "Who is so stupid not to see that the trading companies are nothing but pure monopolies? Even the temporal laws of the heathen forbid them. . . . Kings and princes ought to look into this matter and forbid them by strict laws. But I hear they have a finger in it themselves."

Your misconception may be due to a limited view of Lutheran history. Lutheran immigrants as they arrived in this country concentrated upon the survival of their Lutheran church. Early mission work focused on the nationality of the congregation, so that "Bist du Deutsch?" ("Are you German?") and its Norwegian, Swedish, and Danish counterparts were the priority questions. Given the right nationality, the invitation was extended to join the congregation. When the English language was introduced into Lutheran worship, many argued that Lutheran identity would be lost because the churches would be Americanized.

Lutherans do not exist to promote Lutheranism but to proclaim Jesus Christ. At its truest, Lutheranism varies from society to society as it has throughout its history. As the Augsburg Confession declares: "For it is sufficient for the true unity of the Christian church that the Gospel be preached in conformity with a pure understanding of it and that the sacraments be administered in accordance with the divine Word. It is not necessary for the true unity of the Christian church that ceremonies instituted by humans should be observed uniformly in all places." Evangelical Lutheran Church in America leaders are dedicated to remaining thoroughly Lutheran.

■ Historical background can provide perspective. Most of us tend to think that the church has always been—and always should be—the way we presently experience it. An example of this way of thinking may be seen in the way adults responded to a question in an educational computer program. When the program asked, "Who named the Lutheran church?" they tended to select the answer, "The congregations voted him the honor." When the program responded, "No, congregations were not democratic in those days," they expressed astonishment. They assumed the church was always governed as it is today!

Although we are one in Baptism, there are significant differences that affect our relationships with other Christians. As we seek to reach out to other Christians, there are painful reminders that consciences often do not permit sharing the most powerful and gracious of God's gifts for our lives together: the Supper of our Lord. As Luther reached out to the Orthodox, so the Evangelical Lutheran Church in America sought in its very first year to follow his steps. Bishop Chilstrom's visit to the Orthodox Patriarchate demonstrated both our intentions and the agonies of division. One practice, as reported in *The Lutheran*, puzzled readers and stimulated the following inquiry.

QUESTION When Bishop Herbert W. Chilstrom, head of the Evangelical Lutheran Church in America, participated in worship at the Orthodox Patriarchate in Istanbul, a photo caption in *The Lutheran* (March 2, 1988, p. 7), noted, "Chilstrom receives blessed (but not consecrated) bread from Ecumenical Patriarch Demetrios I." What is the difference between blessed and consecrated bread?

91

RESPONSE Consecrated bread is the bread distributed in communion. The Orthodox also practice a tradition where other bread is blessed and then shared while still at church. This bread may be shared with non-Orthodox Christians.

Although the Orthodox do not celebrate communion with other Christians, partaking of this blessed bread was a way for ELCA and Orthodox leaders to express the unity they share through Christian Baptism. Yet it recognized that significant differences remain to be addressed through prayer and dialog.

■ Greater strains are evident between Lutheran church bodies, especially in the United States, about openness at the Lord's Supper. In areas of the country where Lutheran churches are few and far between, many of the laity will seek out whatever Lutheran church they can find. Furthermore, many have family members who have transferred into congregations of other Lutheran church bodies. When they visit, they want to worship together. When the service includes communion, they wish to receive Christ's gift of grace. They find it difficult to understand when they are excluded from participation at the altar. One questioner had retained membership in her home ELCA congregation but regularly worshiped at the nearest Lutheran congregation. Her conscience compelled her inquiry.

QUESTION Although my membership is with an Evangelical Lutheran Church in America congregation, I currently worship at a Lutheran Church–Missouri Synod congregation. Am I really supposed to believe that I'm doing wrong by taking communion at the LCMS church?

RESPONSE If you mean "sinning" when you say "doing wrong," no. But if your LCMS hosts do not welcome you to the altar, politely respect their wishes. Some congregations will welcome you without reservation. Many in the Missouri Synod believe that in order to commune together at the altar all communicants must agree on all doctrines. They see communion not as a creator of unity but as a sign of unity already achieved.

They are especially careful because of their understanding of Paul's warning in 1 Corinthians 11:27-29: "Whoever eats the bread or drinks the cup of the Lord unworthily sins against the body and blood of the Lord. Let a person examine oneself and then eat . . . and drink . . . as one is eating and drinking judgment on oneself who eats and drinks without discerning the body."

Paul, in this passage, was rebuking Corinthian Christians for taking communion without caring that some members were starving. The Corinthian church celebrated the Lord's Supper within a meal. People brought their own food and ate it themselves. Others were too poor to bring anything and so remained hungry. Paul ripped into this loveless practice and warned them to examine themselves in order to discern the body—the church. The Corinthians' problem was not with the doctrine of Jesus' real presence in the bread and the wine; it was rather with the doctrine of Jesus' real presence in the sister and brother. In chapter 12 Paul further unfolded this reality, proclaiming that if one member suffers, all suffer, for "we are the body of Christ."

In post-Reformation doctrinal disputes this passage was taken to mean that we must believe the doctrine of the real presence when we communed or we could be damned. With the best of intentions this exhortation to care for each other became used to divide us from each other.

It is essential that we correct this harmful misinterpretation. Christ is present graciously for us so "all members may be concerned for one another" (1 Cor. 12:25).

All Lutherans teach that Jesus' body and blood are present along with the bread and wine so people will hunger and thirst for the Lord's Supper.

Since You Answered

We received a full-page answer to our printed response from Samuel H. Nafzger, Executive Director of the Commission on Theology and Church Relations of the Lutheran Church–Missouri Synod. We print it in its entirety here because of its significance. Please note that Dr. Nafzger's letter is responding to an edited version of the above response as it was printed in *The Lutheran*. The printed version, edited due to space limitations, was faithful to our longer answer, although it suggested we were describing the official position of the LCMS. It also did not include some supporting comments that undergird our perspective.

Dr. Nafzger wrote: "I have read with interest the response of Norma and Burton Everist in the April 20 edition of *The Lutheran* to the question of an ELCA member, 'Am I to believe that I am doing wrong by receiving communion at an LCMS church?' I realize the difficulty of presenting in a brief response the rationale of another church body's communion practice, but the answer given in this column seriously misrepresents the official position and practice of The Lutheran Church–Missouri Synod.

"In keeping with historic Christian precedent (cf. 'Closed Communion' in Werner Elert's *Eucharist and Church Fellowship in the First Four Centuries*, pp. 75-83) and the principle set forth in the Augsburg Confession (cf. Article XXIV, 6 'none are admitted unless they are first heard and examined'), congregations of The Lutheran Church–Missouri Synod extend a general invitation only to those individuals who are members of congregations in altar and pulpit fellowship with the Synod to commune at their altars. But this traditional practice, as the LCMS also recognizes, entails 'the necessity of exercising responsible pastoral care in extraordinary situations and circumstances,' including 'the administration of Holy Communion to Christians who are members of denominations not in fellowship with the LCMS' (LCMS Convention Res. 3-08, 1986).

"In following this practice (also followed by the Roman Catholic Church and by the Eastern Orthodox churches), the pastors and congregations of the LCMS seek to be faithful to the biblical requirements presented by St. Paul in 1 Corinthians 11:27-29 that communicants partake of the Sacrament worthily by believing that Christ is bodily present in the elements for the forgiveness of their sins. Neither the presentation of a checklist of doctrines nor the holding up of a fear of 'damnation' are the principal concerns of this traditional practice—as your response seems to imply."

We are pleased to hear of LCMS Convention Resolution 3-08 and its encouragement to pastors and congregations to include nonmembers in communion in extraordinary circumstances. Certainly the pastor who is welcoming the questioner to the congregation's altar is practicing the convention's recommendation.

We also are pleased to agree that the LCMS does not presently hold up the fear of "damnation," and we regret it if that appeared to be our implication. But it is true that post-Reformation doctrinal disputes argued that taking communion without the correct doctrinal understanding of Christ's real presence could result in damnation. The King James Version, upon which many Lutherans in the United States depended, reinforced such opinions as it read: "For he that eateth and drinketh unworthily, eateth and drinketh damnation to himself, not discerning the Lord's body." It is also true that many LCMS pastors felt compelled by their consciences to teach what they understood this passage to say. It is encouraging to see this sad misunderstanding clearly corrected as in Dr. Nafzger's letter.

Nevertheless, Dr. Nafzger's letter exemplifies a doctrinal detour (shared by some other Lutherans, Roman Catholics, Orthodox, and many fundamentalists) that misses Paul's point. Paul is not discussing a doctrinal problem that the Corinthians were debating. Paul is addressing the Corinthian's lack of love for one another, their failure to see and feed people who were in need. The body of Christ Paul wants the Corinthians to see is the body of Christ, the church, and, in particular, the poor who went away starving. When this passage was filtered through the post-Reformation doctrinal controversies surrounding the presence of Christ's body and blood in the bread and wine, all disputing parties missed Paul's point. And much ecumenical dialog continues to miss that point. Put simply: "Look! See your hungry sister and brother! Share with them!"

This is not to argue for casual intercommunion among denominations. Dr. Nafzger's reference to the Augsburg Confession's concern for congregational examination calls for all of us to exercise more thorough care for the spiritual well-being of those who participate in the Lord's Supper. Casual participation of members as well as nonmembers has no place among us. Congregations and the traditions in which they stand exist in order to care for the people of God, to nourish and nurture them so they may discern not only the needs of each other, but the needs of the world as well.

■ In another way the following letter exhibits a misunderstanding of the use of Scripture and doctrine, as a well-intended inquirer searches for ways to persuade Jehovah's Witnesses visitors of the doctrinal truth of the Trinity.

QUESTION When visited by Jehovah's Witnesses or Followers of the Way, I am unsure how to respond to their denial of the doctrine of the Trinity. It would be easier to close the door, but I want to explain the doctrine to them. How do I respond when I point out a Scripture passage and they say, "That's not what it means"?

RESPONSE Former Jehovah's Witnesses confess they did not come to a person's door with an open mind. They came only to convince the listener of a truth of which, they believed, they were the sole possessors. They were not seeking to learn from those who answered the door.

Gently share your faith, decline their materials, and excuse yourself. Then pray for them. Nothing is gained by attempting to prove your understanding from Scripture.

Christian faith is not created through argument or debate. All doctrines exist to equip the people of God for a life of service. Doctrines become meaningful only as Christians live out their faith. The best way to witness to the Jehovah's Witnesses, to the Followers of the Way, or to others is with your life. Your Christian faith can shine through as you work with others, as you join others in life's struggles, as you face social issues in citizens' groups and in political activity, and even as you participate in recreation. You can share your faith as it relates to daily concerns through actions and words.

Since You Answered

One correspondent wanted us to be aware of two publications, *The Kingdom of the Cults* published by Bethany House and *How to Respond to Jehovah's Witnesses* published by Concordia Publishing House.

Two wanted us to respond and witness to the cults, surely an essential task. One writer said, "So many of us Christians feel inadequate in responding to the Jehovah's Witnesses or Mormons on our doorstep because we do not know why we believe in what we believe." This is sadly often true. But witnessing is not the same as arguing or debating. Cult members tend to be "true believers," who have been prepared *not to listen* to whatever we would say.

A simple response, sharing your faith in Jesus Christ as God in the flesh, God's own self given for our redemption, will speak God's love. There are appropriate occasions to bear witness, but attempts to persuade through argumentation—at the door or elsewhere—don't allow for the working of the Spirit.

■ No response aroused more discussion than the one about the Church of Jesus Christ of Latter-day Saints.

QUESTION   We are opening a new church-related facility in Utah. I am concerned that Mormon groups will want to rent it. Should we open our Lutheran facilities to them?

RESPONSE   The Church of Jesus Christ of Latter-day Saints (Mormons) is not Christian, although they use many Christian terms. The Lutheran Council in the U.S.A. studied Mormon baptismal theology and practice and concluded that Lutherans should not recognize baptisms administered in the Mormon Church.

According to the Augsburg Publishing House pamphlet, *Mormonism: An Interpretive Comparison of the Lutheran Church and the Church of Jesus Christ of Latter Day Saints*, which compares Lutheran and Mormon teaching, "the basic beliefs of the Mormon Church are fundamentally different from those of the Lutheran Church, even though the terminology is often similar." For instance, Mormons believe in "salvation by grace," meaning only that everyone will someday be resurrected. Full salvation, however, comes only through obeying the laws and ordinances of the gospel as defined by the Mormon Church.

We need to witness to the fullness of the gospel to individual Mormons. And the Mormon religion deserves the same respect we accord any religion. But since Mormons use familiar language with critically different meanings, it is best to minimize confusion. Permitting official Mormon functions to be held on Lutheran facilities could increase that confusion. Avoid it. However, if your facilities or functions receive federal funding, you may be required to permit use by any group.

Since You Answered

We received responses from Mormons, Lutherans who have become Mormons, people who have Mormon relatives and friends, and some former Mormons (one who still considered the religion a Christian religion and one who had decided that Mormonism was not Christian). Letters were accompanied by extensive literature, much produced by the Church of Jesus Christ of Latter-day Saints itself.

Before we quote some of the writers, let us stress that we regret not saying clearly that it is the *religion* of the Church of Jesus Christ of Latter-day Saints that is not a Christian religion. We could have emphasized that we were not speaking about the faith of individual Mormon members. We do not presume to see into the hearts and faith of individual Mormons, and we ardently hope that, in spite of the official teachings of their religion, they know Christ as God's own self, by whose grace they are not only resurrected, but saved.

One active Mormon wrote: "I am not a Lutheran, but saw a copy of the magazine *The Lutheran* and picked it up to read." The writer claimed, "We *are* Christian," and offered some examples to prove it. Among them was Article 8 of Joseph Smith's (and the Mormon Church's) *Articles of Faith*: "We believe the Bible to be the word of God as far as it is translated correctly; we also believe the Book of Mormon to be the word of God." The writer later expanded, "The Book of Mormon is merely another testament of Christ. It records his appearance to the people of the American continent after his resurrection."

Readers also sent us pamphlets published by the Church of Jesus Christ of Latter-day Saints. While they claim to extol Jesus Christ, it is not as the one who is "very God of very God," but simply the "Firstborn Spirit Child," which can be understood only if we understand Mormon teaching that "all men lived in a pre-existent estate before they were born into this world; all were born in pre-existence as the spirit children of the Father. Christ was the Firstborn Spirit Child, and from that day forward he has had, in all things, preeminence" (from a publication of the Church of Jesus Christ of Latter-day Saints, *What the Mormons Think of Christ*, pp. 36-37).

Most saddening—and alarming—were letters from Lutherans who argued that our Baptism, our understanding of grace, is not important but rather how we live our life. One writer contended, "They are more moral than us Lutherans." We would concede that not only many Mormons but also many others who practice non-Christian religions may be more moral than many Christians. St. Paul rebuffed the Corinthian Christians for not correcting immorality among themselves, immorality that scandalized even the pagan religions. We do not claim superior morality, for the grace of God opens us wide to face our sins, admit them, and seek help in growing more loving in word and deed. This is the meaning of the primary Christian teaching: "For by grace you have been saved through faith; and this is not your own doing, it is the gift of God—not because of works, lest any[one] should boast" (Eph. 2:8-9).

Some writers turned to dictionaries to defend their understanding of Mormonism as a Christian religion. Dictionaries offer secular definitions, and we do not defer to them. Instead we draw our definitions of the Christian faith from the Scriptures and from the ecumenical creeds (Apostles', Nicene, and Athanasian). We also assess the other religions from their official teachings.

Finally, many were concerned that we were being judgmental and that our description was bigoted. In overreaction to intolerance and genuine bigotry, many have failed to see that Christians are called to "discern the spirits, to see whether they be of God." Bigotry includes oppression. We repeat: respect for the religion represented by the Church of Jesus Christ of Latter-day Saints is essential. It is equally essential that we both discern and proclaim the genuine good news of Jesus Christ.

So we encourage close cooperation with other Christians, respect for those with whom we differ, and common venture with all people of goodwill in the public world.

We are also called to grow more caring, to discern what is right, and to do it. This we address in the next chapter.

7

Problems concerning Ethical Issues

Every question about ethical issues printed in *The Lutheran* drew responses from readers; there is much debate about the way we choose to live our lives in the world. Although each issue deals with private matters, the difficulty of decision making relates to balancing an individual's rights with the rights of others. We live in relationships. Are there general ethical principles, or should each decision be based on individual circumstances? Does one pay more attention to one's personal situation or to the community?

In this chapter we weigh issues of life and livelihood, of health and human need. We include a sample of the range of responses to these questions.

QUESTION What biblical references relate to abortion? I'm neither for nor against but feel the decisions should be based on individual circumstances.

RESPONSE The only scripture verse that speaks explicitly about the loss of fetal life is Exodus 21:22, which refers to men causing an injury to a pregnant woman that results in a miscarriage. This passage is set in a patriarchal context in which the value of lives was ranked.

This verse occurs just after rules about slave deaths and barely before oxen. It prescribes a fine as payment for the loss, perhaps because women, children, and slaves were considered property.

Although no Bible passage speaks directly about abortion, many speak directly of the value of all human life and several speak about God's activity in human life prior to birth (Isa. 44:2, Jer. 1:5, Job 10:9-11).

Psalm 139, for example, celebrates God's intimate connection with every human being: "For thou didst form my inward parts, thou didst knit me together in my mother's womb. . . . Wonderful are thy works! Thou knowest me right well."

Scripture speaks not only *against* killing, it also speaks *for* the value of all human life. It is remarkable, given the patriarchal society in which Scripture was written, that New Testament texts show Christ caring about women and their freedom to make decisions. Remarkable, too, is that Jesus honors, heals, and invites children to come to him.

Life is a valuable gift of God. We do no better than the ancient Hebrews if we rank value by the nearness to the time of birth or to the time of death. We are not true to our biblical foundations if we treat lightly the taking of life through war, abortion, or through injustice that produces starvation. The awesome value of all human life is a powerful concept in a "throwaway society."

The gospel calls Christians to live in a complicated world. Legal and scientific possibilities present new dilemmas. The Bible does not free us from making decisions but for living in forgiveness and new life.

The 1980 General Convention of the former American Lutheran Church affirmed "that human life from conception, created in the image of God, is always sacred" and "that induced abortion ends a unique human life." Hence, it deplored "the absence of any legal protection for human life from the time of conception to birth." Similarly the 1978 convention of the former Lutheran Church in America opposed abortion on demand.

Still the statements of both churches acknowledged that there may be circumstances when because of health, family, or societal consequences an abortion may be a "tragic option." This is an alternative to be exercised only after "earnest consideration" and consultation with "physicians and spiritual counselors."

Beyond ministry with those caught up in decisions about abortion, statements from the ELCA predecessor bodies held that the church has a ministry of helping to provide positive measures for preventing those situations where abortion may seem an option. These include "research and development leading to safer, more reliable, inexpensive contraceptives" and "encouraging women and men to share in all parental responsibilities, including child care." They also include "building a sense of fellowship within the congregation to support all people, the family and all its members, the single person . . . the handicapped, the homeless child . . . the woman with an unwanted pregnancy who elects to bring that pregnancy to term, either to keep the child or place it for adoption, as well as the woman who has made the decision to have an abortion. All are children of God; all deserve the church's care, support and acceptance."

Since You Answered

One reader wrote a long letter using Exodus 21:22 to support pro-life advocates. His argument hinged on the word *miscarriage* and whether no harm was done. When all energy is placed on increasing the division between camps—pro-choice and pro-life—not only are people alienated, but positions are hardened. We miss opportunities to care for people. What about a woman who miscarries? When the issue is on "killing," the grief of prospective parents is missed. Women who miscarry suffer. Harm is done.

Another reader asked if abortions are performed in Christian and Jewish hospitals, and went on to say that would be contrary to God's word in Jeremiah 1:4-5: "Before I formed you in the womb I knew you, and before you were born I consecrated you; I appointed you a prophet to the nations." Actually this passage is not about hospitals or health care or abortion or even about birth. It is the well-known word to Jeremiah who was reluctant to become God's prophet.

Yet another reader referred to Exodus 20:1-17, the presentation of the commandments, and related abortion to each commandment, including honoring God's name, stealing, adultery, and coveting. Still another asked that we relieve his "torment and doubt" concerning the church's stand on pro-life issues and abortion. He included a document charging that mainline denominations have diverted millions of dollars intended for mission into "radical causes and militant organizations like Planned Parenthood." This charge is totally false.

The fear and anger of such people is evident. The escalation of violence around the issue adds to the tragedy. Some anti-abortion groups, in the name of "life," have resorted to physical and psychological violence by bombing abortion clinics and by setting up pseudo-clinics staffed by people untrained in medical or counseling skills to convince women to avoid abortion clinics. A more responsible approach is offering support during pregnancy and following birth to both parents and child.

It is important for church groups to carefully study the church's official statements. It is also important to listen carefully to women who have suffered through dangerous, illegal abortions, parents who long to have a child and cannot conceive, women who have miscarried, and medical and social service workers. One woman said, "Pro-lifers don't want to help women have babies, they want to prevent them from not having them."

Life is sacred. Each person is created in the image of God. The sexual union of a man and a woman is holy, and men as well as women need to be part of caring for the unborn child and raising children. Women in historical and contemporary patriarchal societies often have been considered property, with no rights over their bodies or lives. God intends us to care for each person and to seek life. To fearfully, violently "prevent women from not having babies" is to miss the thoughtful, caring, mutually supportive opportunities for ministry that exist all around.

This issue and those that follow raise basic ethical principles. Many say that every ethic is a social ethic; a person becomes a person only in community. Christians say this in even stronger ways. The central words about Christian life are about life together, not about the individual. The question for a Christian is not simply What should I do? but Who am I in Christ Jesus? Loved by God and forgiven, the question is not What do I do to assure my welfare or my righteousness? Placed in Christian community, the question is How do we care for each other and become a servant community in the world? Even in the midst of desperate, lonely situations, with problems that seem overwhelming, we need not, dare not, make difficult decisions alone. We have a *"koinonia* (communal) ethic" that confesses we are a forgiven, serving community. That helps to shape the solution to the What shall I do? questions. We can and should seek the counsel, support, and strength of Christian community, living our lives in mutual accountability. God's unconditional love means we are never alone; God's new life in us enables us to honor God's life in ourselves and to seek life for others.

QUESTION   What does the Bible say about interracial marriage? I do not believe I am racist. The little contact I have had with blacks has been fine. But I am having a difficult time accepting what may become a reality in my family. Please help me understand God's will in a situation such as this.

RESPONSE   The Bible says nothing about interracial marriage, but it is very clear God does not divide people from each other by race. Neither should we. Racism separates people from each other. Do not let it rule you. Beware of its subtle appeal. Racism can cloak itself in appeals to one's "better judgment" and can elevate natural and appropriate concern for the welfare of the couple and their possible children into inappropriate anxiety.

Interracial and intercultural couples do suffer the prejudice of our society. There will be tensions that will require special patience and understanding. Your concerns are not ill-founded. But, since Christ has made us one people, you can prayerfully and graciously support the relationship, even as God does.

Since You Answered

One reader did not disagree with our conclusions but sent biblical passages which she believed spoke about interracial marriage. In Deuteronomy 7:1-3, Moses told the people God's will when they would enter the promised land. "You shall not make marriages with them" is set in the context of not making a covenant with idolatrous nations. It is a warning that such marriages would turn the next generation away from following the Lord to serving other gods. The issue is marriage among different nationalities because in that setting, joining themselves with another nation meant forsaking allegiance to the God of Israel. The reader also referred to two passages about Samaritans, Luke 10:33 and 17:16. She made our point for us. In New Testament times, the Samaritans were a despised, enemy people. Jesus' story of the Samaritan who showed mercy, in contrast to the religious leaders of the chosen people, challenges our prejudice of people foreign to us. Even though they are outside the fold, they may be the source of mercy and care.

Two other readers took exception to our answer. One thought we were insensitive to the questioner. He believed that the woman was appropriately worried about the homogenous integrity of her family, today and after her death. "The marriage will bring dishonor and pain to her family." The second was even stronger. He enclosed sections from a book that claimed: "Negroes and the white race do not have a common ancestry." The logic of the argument goes thus: the "Negro" does not possess the stature of the "white man" and "never will," and that Martin Luther King Jr. knew this because he said the "Negro must attain human dignity." One can easily see the fallacy in that argument, ascribing to the orders of creation the injustices of humankind. The fact remains that centuries of racism are not overcome easily.

Many are troubled about how to use Scripture to make contemporary decisions (as was discussed in chapter 4). Fear keeps people from reaching out beyond previous boundaries and bondage. We then believe we must make decisions that protect families and races and "God's order." Living in the power of the gospel means we do not need to take responsibility for keeping things the way we have been taught they should be, thereby cutting off creative possibilities of reconciliation.

The next question relates to an issue that has become almost a hallmark of "individual rights" in society today. The issue not only weighs the rights of the individual against those of society, but spotlights human life and well-being in relation to the neighbor.

QUESTION After reading that smoking is now forbidden in the Evangelical Lutheran Church in America's churchwide offices in Chicago, I wonder what the attitude of the church is toward smoking and smokers. Is it now felt that smoking is sinful? That smokers are immoral people? That smokers need to be quarantined and ostracized lest they endanger the health of the righteous? Is this crusading good or is it pathological?

RESPONSE Your letter is loaded with emotional words and suggests that you may feel personally ostracized. Ostracizing people is not Christ's way. Crusading—using the cross to hammer people into agreement—is always pathological. This is equally true whether the "hammers" are missiles or words.

It seems clear that smoking is harmful to one's health, which even previously concealed tobacco industry research now shows as it is made public in court cases. We have no commandment saying, "Thou shalt not smoke," but we do have Luther's explanation of the fifth commandment: "We should fear and love God so that we should not endanger our neighbor's life, nor cause our neighbor harm, but help and befriend our neighbor in every necessity of life."

No one is helped if people are labeled immoral. Labeling allows us to ignore people and imagine ourselves superior to them. The spirit with which we help each other deal with any sin, the sin of speeding in traffic, of overeating, of arrogance, as well as the sin of smoking, needs to be a spirit of gentleness and humility. Christians always need to recognize that we all are sinners who need correction, admonition, and forgiveness. No one is righteous except by the gift of Christ.

However, smokers should not require others to smoke with them. This happens when they smoke where the smoke drifts and others must inhale it. This endangers their neighbor's life.

However, the totality of God's law does not allow non-smokers to remain comfortably self-righteous. How do we non-smokers pollute our atmosphere? With our automobiles and our air-conditioning, do we pollute the atmosphere with dioxides? Smokers and nonsmokers all must remain open to challenges to our present way of life and be ready to change if our actions harm ourselves and others. This is the radical never-ending growth to which we are called as disciples of Jesus Christ. The steadfast love of God permits us to grow in this way, for we can admit our sins and be open to change because we live in the forgiveness of sins revealed in Jesus Christ. This cross does not hammer away, but it gently calls us to life.

Since You Answered

One reader took exception to our inclusive concept of sin. "How can you possibly call speeding, overeating, arrogance, and smoking a sin?" she asks. "Must I go into detail of the sins being committed day in and day out by our 'neighbors' and fellow Americans in this corrupt society we live in? *These* are sins and ungodly!" Her anguish showed in her call to "bring back morals, self-respect and decency . . . the way it used to be." The practice of ranking sin is common. It is clear from Scripture and the Lutheran confessions that sin involves fearing, loving, and trusting in anything above God. Sin is anything that hurts our neighbor.

Ranking sin, like ranking "good," leads us to self-justification in relationship to our neighbor and to God. Ranking sin drains energy from the task of caring for the earth and our neighbor. One respondent reported, "Recently the local health department brought it to the attention of our church that smoking throughout the church building, during meetings and social functions, was in violation of local and state regulations. Our council responded quickly to the matter, not wanting to be in violation of the law." In regard to ethics, sometimes people welcome clear civil regulation. It can seemingly "settle the issue." But because Christians, like other citizens, have the power to make and change laws, the difficult ethical issue of weighing individual rights and rights of others remains.

Our response to the original letter addressed the danger of taking an ethical stance that labels and ostracizes. Christian ethics always tries to reconcile communities and form healthy ones. How we do that is difficult to discern. Two readers were diametrically opposed in their comments. One was appropriately concerned that members who smoke may ostracize themselves from church-related activities where no smoking is permitted. She went on to write that, although she as a smoker supports non-smoking areas in public buildings, she questioned studies of the health danger to nonsmokers. "The studies involving side-stream smoke and lung cancer involved spouses that lived together in enclosed areas for many years." She wrote that some studies are being redone because they failed to consider other variables and contaminants, such as the presence of radon gas.

She raised two important considerations for Christians seriously concerned about compassion. She wondered if the loss of power and control over our lives may be fueling the intense "war on smokers." We appear to be losing the wars on drugs, crime, poverty, and pollution, and thus the "war on smokers" provides a cause with some chance for success. Since many smokers became addicted before they were aware it was health-threatening, she urged compassion and understanding for smokers similar to what we are learning to show to victims of AIDS and drug and alcohol abuse.

The other reader accepted the scientific studies of the dangers, adding that tobacco has shortened the lives of more people than alcohol, automobiles, suicide, AIDS, and other behavioral risk factors combined. He agreed that the issue is not morality and condemnation, but helping to free people from tobacco dependence for the sake of a healthier life for themselves and their families. He believed the problem won't be solved without much support and help for those who wish to quit smoking.

In regard to the issue of ostracism, he noted that those allergic to air polluted with tobacco fumes felt ostracized when they could not be in public places because the smoke made them sick. The smoker could still enjoy the public building, save for a needed smoke break; the allergic person could not. The writer concluded, "The moral dimension engages when we affirm an inclusive value and try to create environments where all can come, including the weakest among us."

Having considered questions of life, the following question relates to livelihood.

QUESTION Our congregation takes audiotapes of worship services to our shut-ins, but they miss hearing the music and singing. We would like to include the music on the tapes. Although we erase the tapes when we record another service, current copyright laws appear to disallow taping music for this purpose. Is this correct, or can we play back music?

RESPONSE It is good you are concerned about copyrights. Too many congregations illegally use copyrighted materials without regard for the composers and publishers. A decade ago Christians using copyrighted music material helped bankrupt a religious music publisher because they reprinted music without permission or payment. Such use of copyrighted material is theft as surely as shoplifting is stealing. Some rationalize that they can use other people's work in worship and at camps because they are doing God's work, but God does not condone stealing.

According to Rachel Riensche, director of publication rights and records for Augsburg Fortress, Publishers, the copyright law permits performing music within worship as long as you are using legal copies. Photocopies are illegal unless permission to copy has been granted by the copyright owner.

Recording the service for distribution, on the other hand, violates copyright laws unless permission is given by the copyright owners. Most publishers will grant this permission without charge. Permission to record portions of the liturgy and some hymns in the *Lutheran Book of Worship* may be sought through the publication rights and records department at Augsburg Fortress.

Even after permission is obtained, you might consider setting up teams of visitors who can bring tapes to shut-ins. The visitors could sing the hymns and liturgy with the shut-ins if they feel comfortable doing so, and even bring communion, using the elements from your congregation's most recent service. During the prayers the tape recorder could be stopped to allow time for the homebound and their visitors to offer their own prayers. This is preferable to leaving the tapes or sending sermons in the mail, since it offers more contact with the worshiping community.

Several informative pamphlets on copyright laws are available free from The Copyright Office, Public Information Office, Library of Congress, Washington D.C. 20559. More complete information on copyright issues is available from Copyright Information Services, 440 Tucker Ave., P.O. Box 1460, Friday Harbor WA 98250. A legal-size, stamped, self-addressed envelope to this group will give you a copy of a newsletter that focuses on churches and video copyrights, a related issue. They offer some general information at no charge and several useful publications and tapes. We can, of course, work to change the laws, but until then record only the sermon and the prayer or hymns you know are not copyrighted.

Since You Answered

No one questioned the ethics of the right to pursue a livelihood and no one doubted that illegally using what someone else produced was stealing. Are we in this society more clear on the ethics of products and profits than on life and death?

One person did call for further information because so many churches use tape recordings of services for shut-ins. He had understood the law to mean that *the sale* of such recordings would be illegal, but the temporary use would not require permission of the copyright owner. He reported that choirs sometimes record music during rehearsal for temporary use in learning and thought there was no infringement of copyright unless the recordings were sold or collected in a library. He believed public schools do this with the same understanding. While this may be true, care should be taken to see firsthand the copyright provision and check with authorities before proceeding.

Sometimes new work on Christian ethics must be done simply because new scientific procedures are now possible, raising new questions about the dignity of human life.

QUESTION As a hospital chaplain I am asked to approach people to donate body organs. As Christians we are called to give our lives for the good of others, and this would seem to favor such donations. But since Christ's wounds were part of his glorified body, can we know what effect organ donations will have on our resurrected bodies?

RESPONSE Giving parts of our bodies so others might live more fully reflects the heart of our new life in Christ. It may certainly be encouraged in fitting ways as long as no pressure is exerted. This final opportunity to serve others should not be overlooked. Organ donor cards that specify which organs you may wish to donate can be obtained through many hospitals, doctors, and health organizations. These cards are legal documents and permit your wishes to be followed wherever you may die.

Jesus' resurrection appearances reveal that our bodies will not be bound by the physical laws of creation. In several appearances Jesus was not immediately recognized but was mistaken at one time for a pilgrim and at another for a gardener. Jesus displayed his wounds as he sent the disciples out from the safety of barred doors into a world where they risked being wounded. As the body of Christ, God's people, we are called to be wounded healers in a suffering world. We do not know what our resurrected bodies will look like, but the wounds we might receive by giving our organs, like Christ's wounds, may bring healing to others. If there are scars from such donations, we will not be ashamed of them nor feel disfigured by them. We will be too busy beholding the face of the risen Christ.

Since You Answered

A reader appreciated sensitivity to the issue. "I am the recipient of a donated, transplanted kidney, and have spent the two and a half years since my transplant working as a volunteer organ donor educator for the American Red Cross, and also as a volunteer chaplain at a local hospital." She added two informative points: first, a federal law, which became effective in November 1987, requires all hospitals to provide the opportunity for organ donation to the family members of a person who dies in their facility; and second, if you decide to sign a donor card, it is very important that this decision be shared with your next of kin, because no organs will ever be removed without their consent. Their right to say no will be respected and your organs will not be removed, even if you had wanted them donated. They may also overrule your decision not to donate.

Ethical issues will surface as the world itself changes. Rooted in God's unconditional love and supported by the Christian community, we face new questions together. As the church reaches out to the world, it need not be overwhelmed by the huge task before it. While being the faithful church it is called to be, it will become the servant community in society. We will address questions of the church's vocation in the public world in the final chapter.

8

Ministry in the Public World

We have considered issues of life within the congregation ranging from worship to pastoral relationships, from care to conflict. We have discussed biblical, theological, ecumenical, and ethical matters. We have moved chapter by chapter from sanctuary to classroom to narthex. Now it is time to move beyond the church doors. How does the church decide upon its posture in the public world? Is there a clear mission and ministry in the community and in the world? Do the decisions the public world makes about business, politics, and war and peace concern Christians?

We received the smallest number of questions in this category. Christians care about the world in which they live, but it may be that Christians, at least Lutheran Christians in the United States, often separate issues of prayer and politics. Perhaps they do not have the opportunities and tools to biblically and theologically connect their faith and daily life. It may also be that Christians reflect on their faith in relation to personal ethical decisions for daily life, but doubt that the congregation or the church body should be involved in public issues. Is it because they fear political differences will divide the parish? Is it because of a mistaken understanding of the constitutional separation of church and state? We will explore those issues in this chapter as we look at readers' questions and responses we received. We will add a "Since You Didn't Ask" section, inviting people to think more deeply about the difficult and sometimes dangerous issues of the day, convinced that the Christian church can and must speak and act in the public world.

The first question deals with the issue of church and state. It focused on a symbol, specifically the place of the American flag in worship. The very fact that the question asks for the place of the country's flag *inside* the church building, instead of asking how the church reaches out to the world, may be part of the problem.

QUESTION What is the Lutheran church's position on displaying the American and Christian flags within the worship area? As a veteran of 20 years military service and having served my congregation in almost every office, I am distressed that both flags are not displayed in church.

RESPONSE Your question speaks of your deep devotion to your country and to your congregation. Both are important—and distinct.

It is necessary to ask, What do flags symbolize in the sanctuary? To display a national flag in a place of worship may signify belief in a civil creed or in national values, goals, and actions that may or may not coincide with Christian beliefs. The baptismal font, cross, and empty tomb on the other hand, remind us of the creed of God's unconditional love, suffering, new life, and freedom for servanthood. The national flag symbolizes this country's history, pride, military, and freedom as a form of government.

Many Lutheran congregations, particularly those using the German language, displayed the U.S. flag during World Wars I and II to signify loyalty to the United States rather than to Germany. During the Vietnam War, use or nonuse of the flag made a definite political statement.

By its omission of the subject, *The Manual on the Liturgy—Lutheran Book of Worship* would seem to imply flags are inappropriate in the worship area. The 1965 *Encyclopedia of the Lutheran Church* says: "Neither church flag nor American flag belong strictly to the furnishings of a proper chancel. Use . . . is the discretion of the local congregation." The 1985 *Altar Guild Handbook* states: "National flags, being political symbols that mark the divisions of humankind, do not belong in that space where we celebrate our baptismal oneness. . . . The so-called Christian flag is unnecessary and superfluous in the space were we focus on the altar and cross." Christians may want to use symbols to say God loves people of every land. On special occasions one could display flags of many nations, inviting international students and visitors to participate.

Rather than using the U.S. flag in a worship area, it could be displayed in a room where scouting and other community events are held. Also, as members of this society, we do well to assemble frequently in public places, honoring the nation and its flag, working for justice for all, debating national goals and policies, and ensuring freedom to be safely different together as citizens of the United States. The United States is a pluralistic society. Its symbols belong to people of many different faiths.

You may avoid a tug of war over flags by holding a series of educational forums for members to discuss the meanings of symbols, including our deep emotional attachments to them.

Since You Answered

This was a highly emotional issue, which brought much response. The confusion of terms and concepts complicated the matter. A number noted that they were veterans or had lost a loved one in a battle, adding to the poignancy of the matter. We need to listen with care when people's private lives are intertwined with public and church policy. We cannot, however, back away from difficult decisions. In fact, careful listening and thoughtful response may finally help with a person's deep feelings. Calling another person anti-American or un-Christian is not helpful.

One person wrote to say that flags had been removed from in front of their church without a word and were simply left on the floor of a storage room. Since nothing could be settled in a "dispute" on the matter, two people put the flags back on display. The inability to talk in a constructive manner resulted in individuals simply acting on their own. The silent tug of war, which we mentioned above, might continue back and forth for years. How important it is to listen well, to seek information, to communicate caringly, and to provide a safe environment for a healthy forum so people can listen and learn and decide together.

This same reader felt such issues should be left up to individual congregations and resisted church bodies or seminaries voicing opinions on the matter. He was calling for the very thing his congregation seemed unable to do by themselves. He backed up his argument by saying such matters were "under our rights of the U.S. Constitution." The Constitution, of course, gives citizens freedom of religion. It is this very freedom of religion that gives congregations the right *not* to fly the flag in the sanctuary. Each church body, however, must decide how much latitude congregations have in relationship to the churchwide body. (In this case Lutherans have considerable congregational autonomy but are informed by churchwide guidelines.)

In another letter, *freedom* was used in a convoluted way. "The U.S. flag stands for freedom; without it we wouldn't have the Christian flag and couldn't have the cross and the altar." She concluded, "Our young men are dying for our freedom; what would they think as they attend our churches and see the flags removed?" Yes, men and women die to protect this country's freedoms, and all citizens should respect and appreciate such sacrifice and care for the bereaved. Those who live to return are free to worship where they choose and will be strengthened by the symbols of that religious community.

It is not, however, the American flag that safeguards the cross. Nor is it the nation that enables us to have the church. The freedom of the gospel is a restored relationship with God and freedom from sin, death, and the power of Satan. Such freedom has strengthened Christians living under many varied forms of government, enabling them to confess their faith even under oppression. National freedom to worship where and how we will is a good thing, a principle worth preserving for all. The freedom of the gospel equips people to discern false gods, to work for justice, and to love and care for all people.

Another reader also made some false, but all too common, connections: "Luther's strong emphasis on the state as an order of creation would not seem to me to negate the flag." Indeed Luther had high regard for good government and advocated that the most capable, wise, and just people be in power. However, the church and civil order were much more entwined in Luther's day, and the culture was much less pluralistic. Yet even this fact is not the point. To select Christian symbols for display in Christian worship rather than the U.S. flag is not to negate the flag, but simply to use symbols properly.

One reader ascribed motives to others, a practice that is always dangerous. "I am surprised that Lutheran officialdom is so afraid of the American flag." There is no evidence that leaders of the Lutheran church fear the flag. The same reader believes the church is trying to be "pure" by not having Independence Day on the church calendar. Once again, appropriate separation and clarity of worship symbols and celebrations is the issue.

Perhaps some Christians believe they can keep themselves and their churches "pure" by staying uninvolved in the world. (More letters come to us in this regard in relation to dancing and drinking than in regard to social issues or civil holidays.) In a land where Christians are free to worship as they choose and express their beliefs openly, Christians have a mandate, not to keep their religion pure, but to *keep* their religion by using it in seeking justice and showing mercy in the public world!

Finally, one reader underscored our point: "If the American flag is displayed in church, the flags of many other nations, including some from behind the Iron Curtain, should also be displayed. The church is the fellowship of all believers in Christ, cutting across all national and geographic boundaries."

The following two questions go in quite a different direction. They both deal with the church's ministry in the public world and raise questions of how the church should serve there. Implicit, also, are unspoken but real issues of the "value" of people "outside" the congregation.

QUESTION What is the Lutheran church's position on ministering to the mentally retarded? As a volunteer at the local state hospital, I see other churches holding services for the residents, but not the Lutherans. Some residents have very high IQs. Don't they need the Word of God also?

RESPONSE The Lutheran church has long believed that there is no IQ cutoff point beyond which the grace of God cannot go. God loves all people and all need God's Word. Mentally retarded people need worship services and educational opportunities in which they can fully participate with their abilities and gifts.

For many years Lutherans have been involved in providing homes for the mentally retarded in various parts of the country. In communities with public and private institutions for people with special needs, Lutheran churches have a particular mission opportunity. Even if there are no such institutions nearby, every community has retarded citizens. Congregations that initiate such outreach ministry discover previously invisible people eager to hear God's Word and be part of the worshiping and learning community. Retarded citizens, in turn, enrich the lives of those who have reached out to them. Perhaps you can encourage Lutheran involvement in your local situation by mentioning the needs of the retarded residents to leaders of your congregation.

■ Society has changed a great deal in recent years. Some changes happened because of the witness and ministry of the church, but the church has also learned from the media's more accurate portrayal of mentally retarded people and from such events as the Special Olympics. There still remains, however, in both church and society, fear and misinformation. Some fear residential homes in their neighborhoods. All too frequently, witness opportunities are missed simply through neglect.

The questioner implied another past error. Even in a church body that confesses we are saved by grace through faith alone, intellectual barriers are erected. For years many retarded people were denied Holy Communion because they could not memorize and recite the Catechism. By becoming involved in ministry among retarded people, one soon learns *from* them. That is true of all parish ministry in the public world. One need not fear the stranger nor limit the Word. Having shared the faith, the witness returns renewed.

QUESTION   I wonder if the quilts we make at church really go to the people for whom they are intended. Someone told us we should not make the quilts too pretty or they would end up on the underground market.

RESPONSE   Your group is giving valuable time and energy when you make quilts for relief projects. Your concern is natural and responsible. With so great a need in the world, it is important not to waste resources.

Among charitable organizations, Christian churches have been recognized as the best avenues for giving to the poor. Lutheran World Relief, for example, delivered 249,371 quilts and blankets to the needy in 11 nations during 1986.

Quilts are sent to countries at their request. LWR has one major requirement: a local network to distribute the quilts. The networks put the quilts into the hands of people who need them. They become ponchos, tents, room dividers, stretchers for the sick, as well as blankets.

Quilt making is a special sharing of God's love because it gives joy to the quilters and meets the recipients' urgent needs.

The community of quilt makers is as much a gift as the quilts themselves.

Beautiful, interesting quilts are a joy to make and honor the people who receive them. They become treasures to enjoy as they are put to work. If there is a risk these lovely gifts will be misused, then it mirrors the risk God takes in creating us and giving us the world.

Quilts are always needed. Keep quilting and giving!

■ Christians want to be careful about how they minister in the world. What is the nature of this care? The implied fear in this letter is that the time and energy of the quilt makers would be wasted. The Creator God is caring and orderly, but lavishes beauty on the world, even though some is "wasted" by human beings. Lavishing our love is neither wasteful nor irresponsible. We simply cannot always know how our love and witness will be received.

A similar idea, though not mentioned here, is the judgment that some people in the world are more worthy of our love than others. The resulting fear is not care, but a selfish withholding of ministry. What if someone who is not honest or clean enough receives our gift? Soon that judgment is expanded to include those not of the right color or belief or nationality or political view. We develop a category called "the undeserving" and begin to judge who belongs there. At that point we are reminded by Christ that all of us are undeserving. Forgiveness of sins empowers us to follow Christ into the world to witness and love, and in so doing to learn.

The final question in this section—sent in by readers, that is—deals with an agency of the church.

QUESTION By what authority, moral or biblical, does the leadership of the Evangelical Lutheran Church in America maintain an office for governmental affairs and use that office to promote their personal political opinions?

RESPONSE The ELCA, in accordance with its constitution, has established a Commission for Church in Society that "shall be a means by which this church both listens to and speaks to society." This constitutional mandate directs the commission "to maintain a presence in Washington, D.C., on behalf of the church." The commission is also directed to "carry out this church's advocacy to private sector individuals and institutions."

The Office for Governmental Affairs does not promote someone's personal opinions, but carries out a variety of activities for the ELCA. One of those duties involves contacting legislative offices to express the ELCA's position on issues. Those positions are decided at churchwide assemblies by delegates representing ELCA congregations.

The board of the Commission for Church in Society decided that until the ELCA has generated its own social statements, the basis for advocacy work will be the collection of social statements of the predecessor churches when and only if these statements are in agreement. These statements were approved by delegates to the churchwide conventions of the predecessor churches. The ELCA Washington office does not tell individual Lutherans how to vote, which, besides being beyond its mandate, would be illegal.

Advocacy (speaking out and acting on issues facing society) is part of the church's ministry. Micah 6:8 says, "And what does the Lord require of you but to do justice, and to love kindness, and to walk humbly with your God?" Likewise, the New Testament speaks often about being advocates for the poor.

Advocacy work should not be confused with the work of salvation. The ELCA does not believe it will carry out its work of evangelism through government action nor that people will be saved by the state or by its advocacy.

For information read the ELCA constitution and bylaws, or write to: The Lutheran Office for Governmental Affairs, 122 C Street, N.W., Suite 300, Washington D.C. 20001.

■ The previous question, and the relatively small number of questions about social issues at all, suggests Lutherans may still be more concerned about *whether* they should be involved in the world than about specific issues. Clarity on the biblical mandate for advocacy and action, and power from the gospel may be the thrusts required to engage Lutheran Christians fully in the world. Not that Lutherans are not already in the world. There simply is more need for them to know how to make the connections between their faith and that world.

We insert here some more questions readers did *not* ask us. This time we offer no responses but instead invite you to discuss them with people in the congregation, either in an adult forum or Bible class, or in an informal setting. We encourage you to develop your own responses. This section is followed by some basic helps on "whether" and "how" Christians can be involved in issues in the culture.

Since You Didn't Ask

Spend time wrestling with the following questions. What is the questioner asking? What are the deeper questions behind the questions? What are the fears? The assumptions? How do the Bible and the confessions relate to each? What is the brokenness in each situation? What is the gospel power for new life?

QUESTION I see more and more news features on homeless people in America. I'd like to know the real situation in my own community and region as well as in the nation. Who are these people? What really are the causes? What biblical beliefs are useful here? I would like to be part of the solution to this problem. Where do I start?

RESPONSE:

QUESTION I used to be thankful that my kids weren't exposed to drugs. Now I realize that drug dealers are everywhere. I feel guilty now that it didn't bother me that other people's children in certain neighborhoods of large cities had that environment. The problem seems so big that I feel hopeless. There's always a new drug that seems worse than the ones before. What can Christians and church groups do?

RESPONSE:

QUESTION Last Sunday there was an interpreter for the deaf doing the worship service in sign language. It was beautiful and interesting, but I know we don't have any deaf people in our congregation. What was the point?

RESPONSE:

QUESTION Our evangelism committee struggles with *how* to witness in our community. How can we tell about Jesus Christ in a way that has meaning for people in today's world?

RESPONSE:

QUESTION When I saw a news feature on television about children being gunned down on a playground, I almost cried. Now I read of gangs armed with high-powered automatic rifles and of children being killed in the cross-fire almost every day. What should we do about gangs? Should such weapons be banned?

RESPONSE:

QUESTION A group of people from a nearby Lutheran church are going on a trip to Central America. I don't know what they expect to accomplish there. I believe the president when he talks about the importance of stopping communism in this hemisphere. But I want to do the Christian thing. The issues are so complicated. How can one know what the truth is?

RESPONSE:

QUESTION We live in a very small town, and things are hard with the farm crisis and difficult weather conditions. Now there is pressure again to consolidate schools in the county. I don't know what our town will do without its school. We might as well turn out the lights and all leave. Is there anything our congregation or larger church bodies can do?

RESPONSE:

QUESTION My family lives in the suburbs of a large city. Our church is growing and is friendly enough, but sometimes I think we are slaves to schedules. It's a committee meeting here, practice there. Do we really know each other? We seem caught in a whirl of many worlds, and faith seems to be out of place in most of them. Is going to church and church meetings just one more thing to do?

RESPONSE:

QUESTION Recently the superpowers seem to be getting along better, but I know there are still enough nuclear weapons to kill everyone on earth many times over. I realize God condoned some wars in the Bible, but should Christians tolerate this kind of killing ability?

RESPONSE:

QUESTION A group from our church has been regularly visiting a local nursing home. As we became involved in the lives of the residents, we discovered some hard issues. One man's wife still owns and lives in their home, but she may have to sell it because those assets mean her husband can't get financial assistance for the high nursing home costs. Another woman, we think, is well enough and able to go home, but her children think they have the right to make her stay in the nursing home. We don't know the answers to these questions and don't know what we should or should not do.

RESPONSE:

■ In some of the above questions the person was viewing the world from a "safe" distance. In the final situation, questions arose *because* the parish had engaged in ministry in the world. Each perspective is valid. Actually hearing and seeing about world situations from a distance, strangely enough, may be more dangerous, because without the energy of action one can feel more impotent. But the latter situation has its dilemmas as well.

A congregation sets out to do some relatively "safe" ministry in a nursing home and runs into deeper issues that might even divide the group. They didn't bargain for all these problems! But taking action together and constantly returning to the center of their faith, the cross and resurrection, in worship and study, gives them courage and insight and sustenance for their continuing ministry in the world.

The hesitancy of a parish to become seriously involved in the public world because it's concerned that members will be divided is a valid one. Christians are already out in that public world as used-car salespeople, medical technologists, teachers, farmers, insurance adjusters, real estate agents, custodians, surgeons, social workers, Republicans, and Democrats. The question is not whether they are in the world. The challenge is to find a way to help people connect their faith with the issues they face in those worlds.[1]

Even if parish members seem far apart in what they believe and do, they continue to be members of one body in Christ. One may be working diligently in sales, another in consumer advocacy; two people may be on different sides of a school bond issue. To deny the differences is unnecessary. Christian community and mutual education equips members not only to endure, but to understand and support one another in their divergent ministries in the public world.

As people become more deeply involved in the world, their questions become more complex, but having seen the Spirit alive and at work in and through their lives, they also trust more deeply. It is no longer "we" and "they." The problems of another neighborhood or another country are their own. They see the incarnate Christ present already in that place to which others are afraid to go. They no longer ask whether their faith will be made impure or their doctrine endangered. It is not a matter of entering the world and losing their faith, but of entering the world using their faith.

A Christian community needs boundaries, biblical and confessional as well as institutional, to define who they are. But the Spirit's movement is unrestricted. God is always transcendent and immanent. Grace is always the new possibility of God's saving action, even in a world dancing with death through drugs and nuclear annihilation. A Christian community can trust in the boundless and therefore "boundaryless" activity of a gracious God. The communal life centered on the Word and sacraments, corporate prayer, nurture, and education thrusts people out again to the public realm—not with less conviction—but with greater commitment.

---

1. For an in-depth way to help people with this, inquire about *Connections: Faith and World*, a 30-session adult study using Luther's *Large Catechism* and involving visits to participants' places of vocation. Contact the Division for Congregational Life of the Evangelical Lutheran Church in America, 8765 West Higgins Road, Chicago IL 60631; 312-380-2700.

The boundaries are not rigid and doctrinaire but are shaped as the church responds to the ongoing call to minister in the world. Accountability is not to a set of rules but to the body of Christ. The gospel transforms the distrust that builds more boundaries into a trust that God is already at work in the world. Faithfulness means trusting a God who gives identity and calls Christians into the world, not to lose their identity, but to live it. The church is empowered for servanthood in God's public world.

There are many more questions. We will continue to care about our corporate life of worship and be perplexed about our propensity to hurt each other in our relationships within congregations. We will grow and change throughout our lives. We will need to wade more deeply into the waters of Baptism and search further in biblical and theological study. We will want to listen and learn ecumenically and struggle ethically. All the while the God who has joined us as one in the body of Christ holds us in God's love. We can, therefore, continue to question and respond. We're glad you asked!